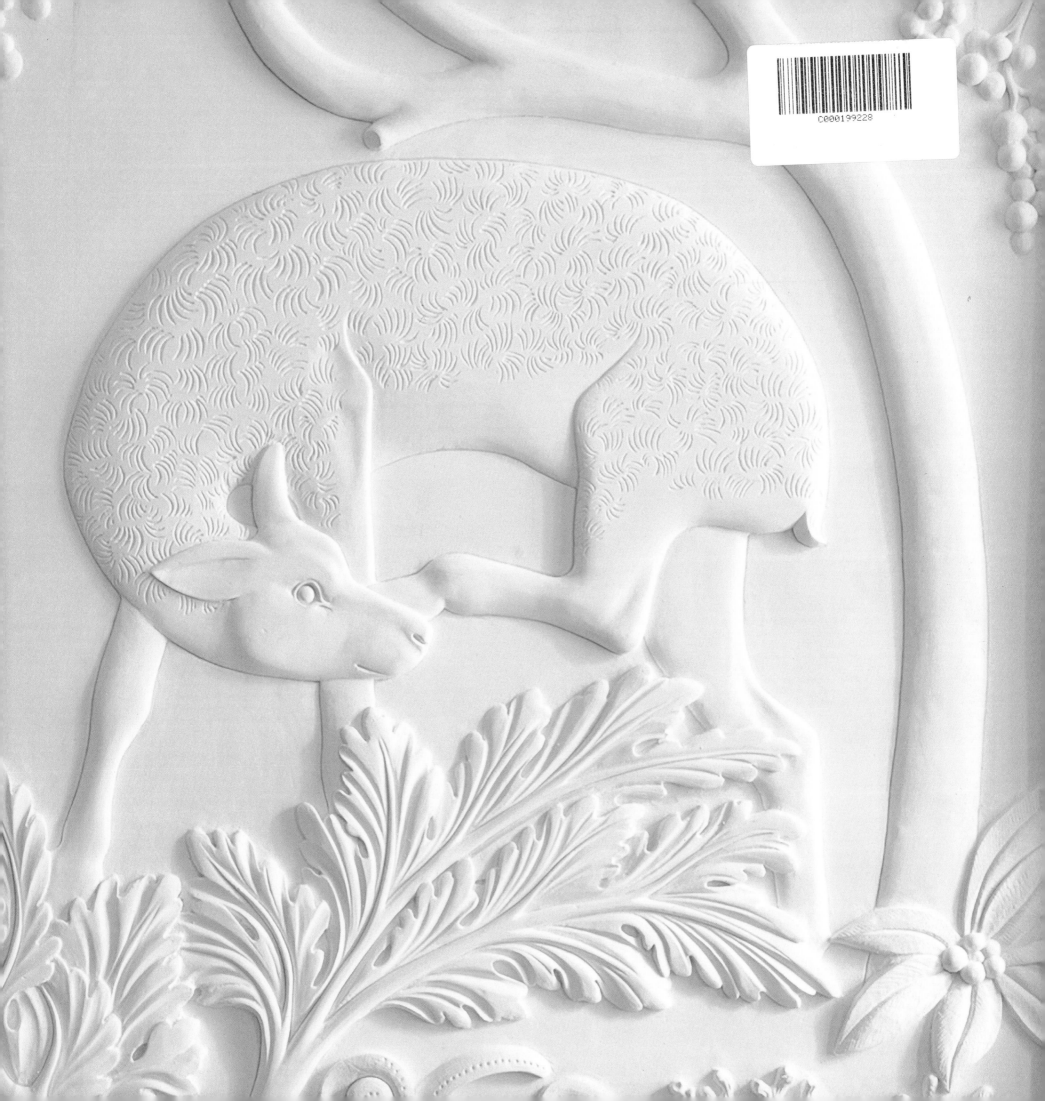

LUMINOUS INTERIORS

BRIAN J. McCARTHY

LUMINOUS INTERIORS

BRIAN J. McCARTHY

WRITTEN WITH MARC KRISTAL
FOREWORD BY BUNNY WILLIAMS

STEWART, TABORI & CHANG | NEW YORK

I DEDICATE THIS BOOK TO MY WONDERFUL CLIENTS (WHOSE PRIVACY I RESPECT—YOU KNOW WHO YOU ARE) WHO ENTRUST IN US THEIR CONFIDENCE TO SEE THROUGH THEIR EYES AND ALLOW US TO MAKE THEIR DREAMS COME TRUE AND BELIEVE IN OUR VISION TO HELP SHAPE THEIR LIVES. THEY ARE TRULY THE PATRONS OF OUR ART.

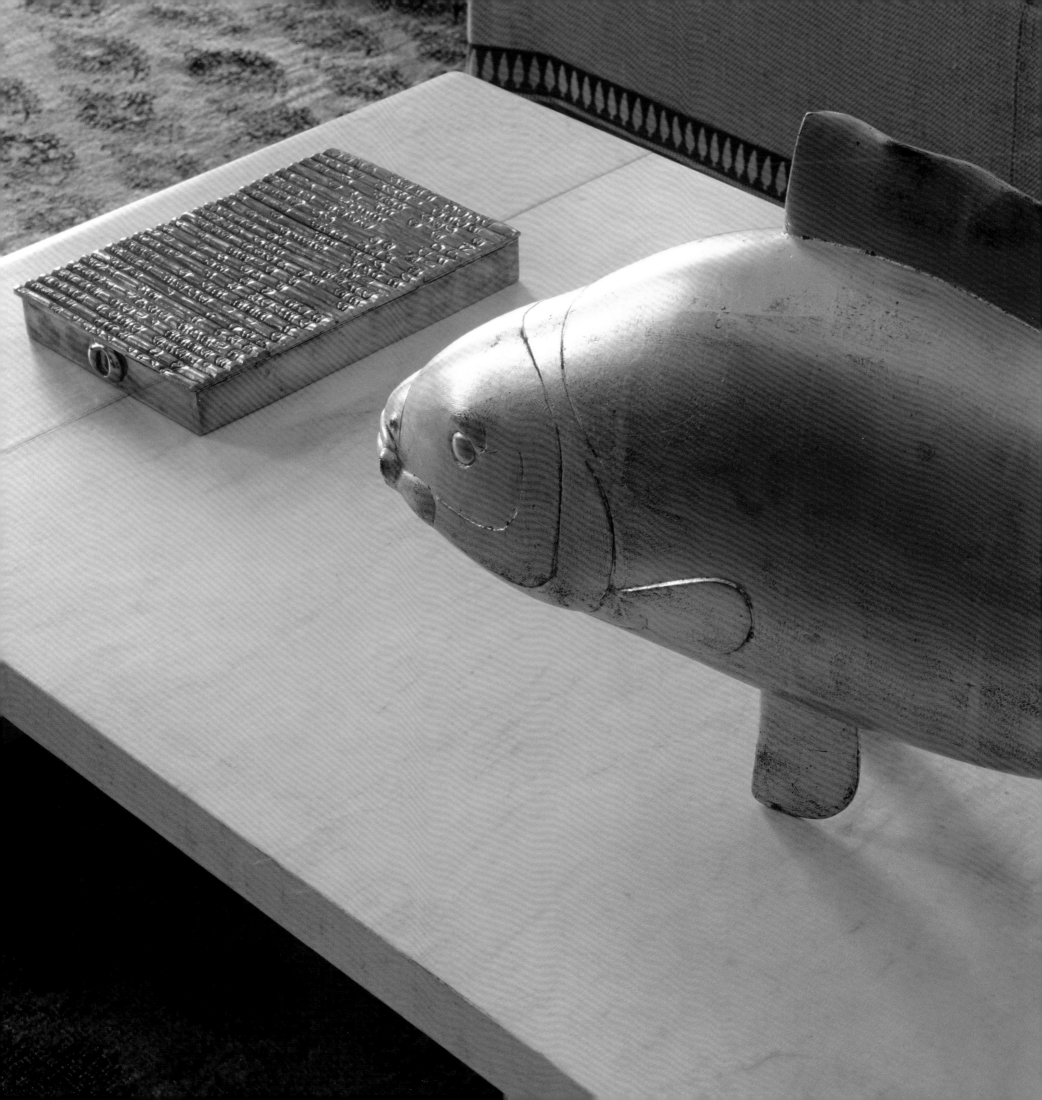

CONTENTS

FOREWORD

In the early 1980s, a very tall handsome twenty-three-year-old young man, a recent graduate of design school, applied for a position at Parish Hadley, where I was one of the senior designers. Needing help desperately on my projects, he was given the job of my assistant. His name was Brian McCarthy. Coming fresh from design school, his idea of a color scheme was various shades of mauve, but within weeks the most beautiful fabrics and trims began to appear in the office after his shopping expeditions. Albert Hadley soon saw his amazing potential and took him under his wing to assist him on his projects. This was the beginning, but it was Brian's passion for design and all the decorative arts, his passion for architecture and art that has made him the great designer he is today.

The richness of Brian's work comes from a curiosity and knowledge of all periods of design. He is a constant student: reading, traveling, absorbing the best, and, in the end, creating his own interpretations. He has traveled the world seeking the greatest artisans, whose work he incorporates into his projects. He has an incredible eye and passion for art, always seeking new talent. Because of this knowledge his projects are always unique and the variety is that of a truly great designer.

Recently, Brian, David Kleinberg, and I have come together on various occasions to celebrate the life of Albert Hadley. It has been like siblings finding each other after a period of time and having the most wonderful moments talking about and exploring our upbringing. Like Albert, Brian's body of work is brilliant, innovative, and timeless, and will be an inspiration to many for years to come. This book will become a classic.

—*Bunny Williams*

9

INTRODUCTION

Though I've had my own interior design firm since 1991, the nine residences selected for this book were all completed within the last six years, and represent the crystallization of my particular design vision: the direction in which I've begun to move (and the variety of styles I employ), after more than thirty years on the job, as a mature practitioner of my craft. Yet the process of selection—of going back and scrutinizing dozens of projects, and considering each in the context of a larger body of work—has reminded me that what I do today is the outcome of a long process of discovery, a creative and personal voyage that reaches back in time to a largely vanished world, and has taught me invaluable, and occasionally unexpected, lessons.

Surprisingly (even to me), while I always had a lively interest in houses, and an even greater one in art, I never had the slightest intention of doing what I do today. My desire was to be on the back of a horse: I began show jumping at the age of ten, and continued for nearly forty years; I confess I would have loved to have been an Olympian. But my parents, a naval architect and a social worker, didn't consider "horseman" to be a proper profession, and, after spending a year full-time on the equestrian circuit after high school, I didn't believe it was the life for me, either. My academic record was pretty undistinguished, but riding had taught me that if I applied myself to something, I could be good at it. So I put my confidence in my drawing and painting skills and decided to tackle art school.

Pratt Institute in Brooklyn, which I loved the moment I arrived for my admissions interview, proved to be the perfect environment. When I started, I had the idea that I might want to be an industrial designer. But your "foundation" year at Pratt is structured to offer a comprehensive introduction to all of the institution's departments, and once I saw what the interior design classes were all about, the prospect of

In my New York office, a painting by Kati Heck hangs above a Jean-Michel Frank–inspired marquetry mantelpiece executed in mirror. The bookcases (an identical one is on the other side of the fireplace) are of my design.

reinventing the electric toothbrush quickly lost its appeal. I became fascinated instead with developing *ways of life*—of creating original worlds people could inhabit gracefully, in sync with their personalities and needs, and, not least, with style.

I loved the work and, applying myself, started to be good at it. But it wasn't until the second half of my junior year that I began defining my own perspective, in a manner that differentiated my approach from those of the other students. At the time, enthusiasm for postmodernism was at its peak; I drew on the movement—its embrace of difference, its lack of certainty about what does and does not constitute good design—but wanted to take it further by introducing a measure of eclecticism into the postmodern vocabulary: eighteenth- and nineteenth-century elements that resonated in a contemporary decorative environment without extracting light-spiritedness or comfort. By my senior year I was, by the standards of the day, a true subversive: visiting antique shops and galleries in Manhattan, and getting to know the dealers, who opened my eyes to new realms of possibility.

Upon graduation in 1983, I was lucky enough to land a job at Parish-Hadley Associates, one of the most influential interior design firms of its time, founded by two legendary principals—Sister Parish and Albert Hadley—who came out of entirely different traditions that each made very much their own. Sister's style belonged to patrician England, to which she added an American twist, bringing things like patchwork quilts into classical interiors and leavening their formality with a welcome whimsy. Albert, conversely, was a modernist whose antecedents were Jean-Michel Frank, Van Day Truex, and, later, Billy Baldwin; he was a patient, thoughtful listener whose designs were at once shot through with excitement and entirely, blissfully livable. Whether working separately or together, Sister and Albert captured the eclecticism I so appreciated. They were never rigid in their handling of materials or styles, but rather mixed the things they loved surprisingly and without the slightest hint of the academy's chill.

I was fortunate, too, to have gone to work when I did, as the interior design world was very different back then than it is today. There were fewer firms—the ones that existed mostly had long, colorful histories—and the business itself was quieter: less aggressive, more genteel. The nature of the clientele, too, at least at Parish-

Hadley, was different. Those who knocked on Sister and Albert's door came from families that had worked with decorators, often the same ones, for generations; as people who understood that interior design is a craft, our clients back then tended to be less overtly demanding, and more attuned to the idea of a creative process that involved trial and error, give and take. Don't misunderstand me: the individuals I collaborate with today (as you'll discover in the pages to come) are exceptionally generous in their trust, and involve themselves in the work with energy and imagination. But times have changed, and in the high-pressure, big-money environment of the present day, people sometimes treat decorators as service providers and nothing more. I was fortunate to come up at a time when clients allowed us to find our way to the richness and subtlety that elevates an interior from the well-done to the magical.

It's true as well that I learned from those early clients, in ways that have had a lasting impact on my approach. Because they'd worked for decades with decorators, frequently on grand-scale homes with complicated programs, these people, as the saying goes, knew the drill, and showed me what a major residence requires in order to run smoothly. These days we often encounter clients who've done very well very quickly, and want to celebrate their success with a showplace home—close in spirit to a boutique hotel—without quite knowing what goes into making it work. Thanks to my Parish-Hadley education, I can help them come to terms with how a home needs to flow, and ensure the essential building blocks are in place.

Once I launched my own practice, I began using these and other lessons to tell design stories that are particular to my office, while at the same time avoiding the trap of creating a "branded" look and applying it repeatedly. Fortuitously, the most important thing I learned virtually guarantees that while there's a thread that runs through everything, no two projects are ever alike: *It's all about the homeowner*. That's why the first step always involves spending time with a client so we can get to know one another—looking at images, visiting museums and galleries, developing an ebb and flow that enables us to see through each another's eyes.

Having established a promising collaborative relationship, I progress, not to decoration, but to a residence's bones: working with a client's architect to improve details, proportions, and plans. Though there are decorators who concern themselves primarily with what goes into a room, once the architecture is in place, I invest a great deal of creative imagination in developing the backgrounds for each space, pushing the level of finish until it's as distinctive, specific, and dynamic as I can make it. This goes well beyond selecting paint colors or wall coverings, and can involve teams of artisans experimenting with materials for extended periods of time, which is why a sympathetic client remains essential—the process is not for the faint of heart. But when you've got it—when the idea or concept has been transformed into surfaces that are truly unique—you have a house that's alive with personality before you've put a single object into a room.

That distinctiveness, that highly particular envelope, sets the tone for the furnishings. While I don't necessarily need to find a single object to inspire an entire design scheme, three facts typically come into play: I am drawn to quality, not for its own sake, but for the craft and originality that underlie it; an object's sculptural aspect, the way in which it establishes itself and holds its own within a room, is as important to me as its function; and if a furniture piece is especially strong, it will influence everything that shares its environment. I always begin with a very tight furniture plan, showing what will be in a room, and how it will all work together. But as the pieces start falling into place, their significance creates an authority that is as distinct as that of the finishes.

I've always had a knack for drawing and painting, yet I knew, when I started at Pratt, that being a fine artist wasn't for me—I didn't have the passion or personality. Even so, I remain a committed collector and, especially in the last decade, art has informed my work and life on multiple levels. It plays a critical role in the interiors I design and, by enabling me to inhabit a prismatic and sophisticated cultural environment, has led me to do very different things stylistically than I might ever have otherwise considered. And though I could never spend my life alone in a room painting pictures, I suppose I have an "artistic temperament" in one crucial respect: the canvas that is an interior is one on which nothing goes unnoticed, and everything has to be properly, completely done before I will consider it finished. I am unapologetically a perfectionist, and firmly believe that once my clients and I have developed a vision, we need to carry it through to completion in every particular—and not compromise on the details, or settle for something less than what we want, or run out of steam before we cross the finish line. I don't mind doing less properly rather than more poorly. I am happy to organize a project in stages, so that we accomplish specific goals over a set period of months or years, in order to give clients the time they need to tackle different elements. Creating an interior design is like building a great art collection: it can require as long as a decade to find just the right piece, the dream object that is elusive but essential. As long as the finished picture expresses that which we saw in our mind's eye at the outset (or better), I know I've given the work my very best.

This perspective, I admit, is the outcome of a long process of evolution and, indeed, maturation. Today, the painter Willem de Kooning is someone I deeply admire. Yet when I was at Pratt, and heavily into Impressionism, I remember going to a big de Kooning retrospective and thinking, "This looks like something I'd have done when I was a kid." The work I produce today involves a monumental amount of detail, and there's always a moment when I ask myself why I've chosen to make things so difficult for my office. The answer is that I've grown, over three decades, into an understanding of what I hope to achieve with every project, and what's required to get there—and the truth is, I'm very grateful for it. That's the voyage I spoke about—the voyage of life: growing, changing, becoming at once a better person and better at what I do.

In a way, I suppose I'm still on the back of a horse. What I loved most about riding was the union between the animal and human: in order to be successful, I had to learn how to create a good relationship between the two, because it's the unity of your own spirit with that of the horse that enables the pair of you, as one, to win. The most important thing you learn in riding is sensitivity to temperament, and this has of course been invaluable to me in working with clients (I always say that I'm really good at defusing a bomb). Yet playing a sport that requires communion between two different kinds of beings has been beneficial in another sense, as what might be described as our "animal" nature is very often the repository of our artistic side. To be able to combine the intellectual and intuitive, theory and inspiration, the process of creation and the need to achieve a result—and to ride it all to victory—represents the essence of my experience as a designer. It is a journey that, from the beginning to the present, has been one I can smile about and be proud of, and hopefully it always will be.

URBAN GRAPHIC

I'M VERY FORTUNATE TO HAVE SPENT MUCH OF THE FIRST DECADE OF MY PROFESSIONAL LIFE AT THE LEGENDARY INTERIOR DESIGN FIRM PARISH-HADLEY ASSOCIATES, BEGINNING AS AN ASSISTANT TO ALBERT HADLEY (1920–2012)—NOT ONLY THE LOVELIEST OF GENTLEMEN AND AN INCOMPA-RABLE TEACHER, BUT, IF I MAY SAY SO, ONE OF THE MOST IMPORTANT AND INFLUENTIAL DECORATIVE ARTS FIGURES OF THE LAST CENTURY. IT WAS A SPECIAL PRIVILEGE, AND A NOT INCONSIDERABLE CHALLENGE, WHEN I WAS ASKED TO DESIGN THIS 6,000-SQUARE-FOOT FLOOR-THROUGH APART-MENT ON MANHATTAN'S UPPER EAST SIDE, AS THE PREVIOUS OWNERS HAD ENGAGED ALBERT TO CREATE THEIR INTERIORS.

It was, in many ways, an exciting and promising project, beginning with the apartment itself. With windows on all four exposures (including extensive glazing on both the living room's north and south sides), there was never a time of day when it wasn't light and bright. The place offered the sort of clear separation between the public and private zones you'd expect to find only in a private house. And though my clients would have preferred the ceilings a foot or so higher, they were delighted to have discovered a home that was so comfortable, family friendly, and gracious for entertaining.

Albert's approach to the design had been to leave the apartment more or less as he'd found it architecturally, and to create very elegant Park Avenue–style rooms. That turned out to be a positive for my clients, as they were coming from a Park Avenue "dowager" and lived in their new place for nearly a year before making any substantive changes—a trial period in which they had an opportunity to experience their residence intimately, and decide how they wanted it to be different.

Fortuitously, though he's fairly traditional in his tastes, and she's got a more modern vibe, the two are excellent communicators and adept at making mutually satisfying decisions. And what they decided they were after was a blend of his authority and her vitality: a sophisticated, present-day New York glamour, as opposed to the old-line style with which they'd been living—in effect, a modern take on tradition.

I found myself entirely in accord with this approach and had a strong sense of how to bring it to life, one rooted, in a way, in the past. One of Albert Hadley's great talents lay in his ability to create surprise: to ring a delightful, sometimes audacious change on expectation that could make what might otherwise have been a very traditional room crackle with excitement. Perhaps the best example of this remains the red lacquer and brass library he created for Brooke Astor in the 1970s; the concept, which replaced a Louis XV–style boiserie chamber (within a very proper Park Avenue apartment and building), managed to be at once classic and

PREVIOUS: In the gallery of this New York apartment, we worked with the architecture firm Fairfax & Sammons to transform the space, introducing a vaulted ceiling, running-key frieze, and herringbone-patterned floor. A seventeenth-century Dutch mirror hangs above a black lacquer and gilt eighteenth-century Italian commode. The appliqué on the Empire chair's seat cushion is my ode to designer Emilio Terry. Painting by Helen Frankenthaler. OPPOSITE: A work on paper by Richard Serra in the entry. The white lacquer walls are soft and smooth yet luminous.

ABOVE: A 1950s Louis XVI–style desk by Jansen, atop a custom top-stitched calfskin rug, in the living room.
OPPOSITE: All of the architectural details—the faux-painted pilasters and capitals, panelized ceiling, cornice, and frieze—
are new. A Milton Avery hangs on the mirrored wall opposite the fireplace. Rock crystal lamps flank the sofa.

OPPOSITE: A canvas by Henri Lebasque (1865–1937), above a silvered eighteenth-century Italian table. I set a Lucite piece before the sofa, to contrast the modern material (in the form of a clear silhouette) with all the lacquer and glass.
ABOVE: A second Lebasque, in a niche that previously held bookcases; the gilded iron coffee table is by Maison Ramsay.

stunningly of the moment—and, for that client and context, utterly surprising—and remains one of the icons of American interior design.

I have always emphasized, in my own work, the idea of layering: bringing together interior architecture, finishes, furniture, art, and decorative objects and elements in a well-modulated yet rich experience that, with its elegance and abundance, really gives a home a heart and soul. But layering, especially when it involves mixing the contemporary and traditional, as my clients proposed to do, is also an excellent way to create surprise, of the sort that (like Mrs. Astor's library) makes an interior stand *en pointe*—and that's what I envisioned for this apartment.

A large amount of the decorator's craft involves architecture, and that has never been more the case than it was here, at every scale. The biggest changes involved the kitchen, in which we reapportioned the space and shifted the elements to create a very capacious and comfortable, sunlit room for cooking, informal dining, and hanging out; and the master suite, previously a needlessly complicated warren of little rooms and circuitous hallways that was simplified and reorganized (enlarging the bedroom in the process). And, collaborating closely with the classical architecture firm Fairfax & Sammons, we changed the casings, capitals, cornices, and other details throughout the entire residence, to give the place a unity—a voice—that drew on nineteenth-century England, almost as though we were designing a Regency town house. That Regency Revival glamour, with its clean lines and light hand, pairs beautifully with furniture from the 1920s and 1930s, and enabled us to build a bridge between the crisply traditional and the "classically" modern. (We also inserted a very slight but significant circulation change, by creating a portal that enabled the living room and library to communicate directly with each other.)

Within the spaces themselves, I pursued specific architectural changes that particularized their character and punched up (to use a proper design term) their impact. The entry gallery needed a bold, graphic element,

A sleigh-style Empire chair faces an extraordinary *Banc Crocodile* bench by Claude Lalanne. When my clients asked me, "If you could choose any coffee table in the world for this room, which would it be?" I unhesitatingly replied, "This is it!" The portal at right, opening onto the living room, was previously a bookcase; the light-filled enfilade completely changed the room's character.

to set a tone of high-key glamour, and so I installed a two-tone herringbone floor, set within a Greek key border, made from black walnut and white oak; above, the flat ceiling was exchanged for a barrel vault finished in 22-carat gold leaf, which individualizes the entry experience and adds a sumptuous glow. In the big rectangular dining room, we added concave niches (incorporating mirrors and cabinetry) in the corners, which broke the plan's rigid grid and made the space more interesting, more pleasing to the eye. We also essentially reconstructed the living room, bringing in a series of pilasters (faux painted to resemble Macassar ebony) topped by capitals, which give it a forceful rhythm; the newly paneled ceiling and framed articulated niches flanking the fireplace reflect Fairfax & Sammons's meticulous perfection of the room's proportions.

The library remains the only room to which we made no physical alterations, other than adding the portal; but it did get the apartment's most unusual surface treatment. As it was originally paneled in a very dull pine, I wanted to invest it with a richness on the order of the queen's bedchamber at Ham House outside London, which I'd always admired, and we decided to faux paint the walls to resemble mahogany. But with a twist: regularly spaced "knots" of the sort you'd find in book-matched panels, with undergilding to give them a dimension of luminosity. When my clients arrived one day to find a team of artisans applying what resembled a series of golden doughnuts to the walls, they reacted with a not-inappropriate skepticism—but the outcome is a sumptuousness that's surprising in so proper a room.

Certain of the decorative elements, too, were chosen to knock things a bit off-kilter. Each room has a judiciously selected mixture of antique and modern pieces, and the palettes were kept simple (claret, green, and brown in the library, for instance; coral, crème, and brown in the living room). But each space showcases something more unbuttoned in spirit. On the black lacquer eighteenth-century Italian commode in the entry, I set a strongly surrealist lamp, by a contemporary Parisian artist, in the form of a headless figure. Rather than a traditional rug in the living room, we created a "younger" one from squares of calfskin in

A pair of English Regency rosewood consoles flank the fireplace; two Directoire chairs
by Jacob stand on either side of a Regency trictrac table. The painting is by Philip Guston.

Inspired by the queen's bedroom at Ham House outside of London, the library's pale pine panels are faux-finished in a rich mahogany; the overscaled "knots" were undergilded to give them greater exuberance (I also gilded the egg-and-dart motif in the cornice, for an extra bit of levity).

To prevent the dining room from becoming overfurnished, and to distinguish it from the residence's uniformly rectilinear rooms, I added inward-curving cabinets at each corner, mirroring them to introduce an element of reflectivity. The sideboard, a circa-1928 piece by Sue et Mare finished in burled walnut and mahogany, makes an especially strong statement; the appetite-inducing sixteenth-century Dutch genre painting is illuminated by a pair of 1940s Regency-style sconces.

shades of sand and cream (a Lucite table from the 1970s, among the more substantive furnishings, introduces the immaterial). A Jean Arp sculpture atop a Macassar pedestal, standing before the dining room window, makes a wonderful silhouette against the glass and pits its sinuousness against the brick wall that forms the view. And in the library, an extraordinary bronze Claude Lalanne coffee table, in the form of a crocodile enveloped by reeds, upends the space's traditionalism with its crazy exuberance.

The master bedroom, which to me conveys a contemporary version of classic Hollywood glamour, also has a simple palette, with white Venetian plaster walls and furniture finished in black lacquer, its elements unified by a quiet fretwork-patterned rug that doesn't detract from the strength of the pieces within the space. The element of surprise comes from, of all things, a zebra head, mounted on a corner wall beside the French windows. I could excuse its inclusion by saying that the creature has been with the family for years (it has), but the truth is that I love taxidermy, the strength of the silhouette against the plaster is exceptionally striking—and a zebra head in an Upper East Side bedroom is the very definition of unexpected.

Though the apartment is all about the clients, I confess that I myself feel very comfortable, very much at home, whenever I visit. Your senses are heightened in a pleasing way—there's a lot to take in visually, but it's not a mental jumping-jacks exercise; everywhere you sit, you discover something that's not immediately apparent, a process that is, paradoxically, quite restful. If I have one regret, it's that I never had a chance to walk Albert through it. I think he'd have approved: The design reflects his way of seeing things and continues the Parish-Hadley legacy in a new-century manner.

Fortuny, as the family's much-beloved zebra head is named, hangs in a corner of the master suite. The fretwork-patterned carpet introduces a vitalizing element into a simple, predominantly black-and-white experience. The custom-designed paisley curtain and chair fabric, with its Anglo-Indian influence, connects graphically to both the zebra skins and the rug.

ABOVE: The fireplace was originally in the living room; its mirrored overmantel opens to reveal a television. A pair of Venini vases sit atop a 1950s commode. OPPOSITE: The lady's master bath, finished entirely in marble, features a mirror set into translucent glass in front of the windows, which fill the space with natural illumination.

CLASSIC GLAMOUR

IN THE DECORATIVE ARTS (AS IN SO MANY WALKS OF LIFE), IT'S VERY OFTEN TRUE THAT PEOPLE WON'T HIRE YOU TO DO A JOB UNLESS YOU'VE DONE *PRECISELY* THE SAME THING BEFORE. THIS HAS TO DO, OF COURSE, WITH THE DESIRE TO FEEL MORE SECURE ABOUT THE CHANCES OF A SUCCESSFUL OUTCOME, ESPECIALLY IF THE SERVICE TO BE DELIVERED IS A CREATIVE ONE THAT CAN'T BE QUANTIFIED. SO I WAS FORTUNATE, IN THIS CASE, TO BE WORKING WITH A COUPLE WHO, THOUGH THERE WAS NOTHING I'D DONE THAT MATCHED PRECISELY WHAT THEY WANTED, RESPONDED TO MY OFFICE'S SIGNATURE ATTENTION TO DETAIL, MY OWN APPRECIATION OF MODERN AND CONTEMPORARY ART, AND OUR ABILITY TO BRING TOGETHER PIECES FROM DIFFERENT PERIODS AND CENTURIES IN A MUTUALLY ENRICHING DIALOGUE. MY CLIENTS AND I WERE ALSO SIMILAR IN OUR TASTES, THOUGH, TO MY CONSIDERABLE BENEFIT, WE CAME AT THINGS FROM DIFFERENT DIRECTIONS.

The couple had a very strong notion of what they wanted, evident in the white-painted brick residence designed by Robert A. M. Stern (with project architect Randy Correll): Inspired by the work of David Adler, the architecture had a lightness and restraint about it, a clean-lined classicism that harkened back to late 1930s Hollywood and showed an easy, natural glamour. That quality was precisely what my clients hoped to capture in the interiors—and to do so in the pale pastel palette that was their preference, as opposed to dialing things up, which would have been my inclination. Thus the task became one of devising different interpretations of glamour within the architecture's light-handed context—and to work in a different way, which proved to be an excellent education.

In the long entry hall, which also serves as an occasional entertainment space and full-time gallery—home to large-scale works of art, and a pair of slender Serge Roche pedestals—glamour was achieved by minimizing decorative elements to foreground the architecture's grand elegance, as well as by a fantastical alteration of scale in the form of a huge steel sculpture, set within a sweeping staircase, that contrasts wittily with its traditional surroundings. There's also a sprinkling of the surreal: a pair of tables of my design that, at a glance, appear to be classically draped consoles but are actually sculptural objects made of plaster-coated resin—a 1930s-style, Roche-inspired element that's very twenty-first century.

Extracting the color from a space, so that virtually all that remains are the outlines of objects and motifs, can be as chic as a diamond necklace sparkling against pale skin; that was the effect we sought in the formal dining room, which is enveloped in a silvered rice paper on which the birds and butterflies show only blushes of pink and blue. Contemporary tree-form consoles derived from eighteenth-century English models extend the tracery into three dimensions and rest discreetly against the walls, deferring to the white neoclassical dining chairs silhouetted against the ebonized floor.

PREVIOUS: In the entry, an eighteenth-century Danish walnut and gilt commode sits below a nineteenth-century Bohemian mirror in the Venetian style; the chairs, by Jacob Frères, date from the early nineteenth century.
OPPOSITE: In the long entry hall, one of a pair of consoles of my design, executed by the artist Bill Sullivan in a plaster-coated resin. A painting by Anselm Kiefer is paired with an antique Chinese terra cotta horse.

ABOVE: A pair of torsolike Serge Roche objets flank the entrance to the library. OPPOSITE: The library's ninety turquoise Chinese lacquer panels were fabricated in the United States, then sent to Paris for finishing; the banding is gilt bronze. The book-matched zebra rug is made from hides with complementary colors and patterns.

The turquoise, ivory, and ash-brown palette is equally beautiful by day or night. The double doors on either side of the black marble fireplace open onto the adjoining loggia.

43

The living room, with Alice Neel's idiosyncratic portrait of Mr. and Mrs. Red Grooms above the fireplace, is one of the home's quietest rooms, and it summons glamour in appropriately discreet ways—through exquisite tailoring, small transgressions of expectation, and refined detail. The design grew out of the need to prevent the existing furnishings from creating an atmosphere that might tend toward the old-lady. We retained the old sofa, tightening up the pillowed back and giving it a more shapely profile; added club chairs of my design, with gilded lotus-leaf feet and superbly handcrafted upholstered scrollwork, which are as unique as bespoke couture; and brought in gilded eighteenth-century armchairs and coffee tables in the style of Jean-Michel Frank and Jean Royère. A carved and gilded molding detail, setting off the entry portal, fireplace, and windows (and reinterpreted in the embroidery on the curtains), contributes as well to the multiple discreet tweaks that turned a potential dowager into an ingénue.

Though it measures a scant six by fifteen feet, the book room, off the second-floor master suite, is one of my favorites for the way in which it treats classical detailing and proportions in a very contemporary, almost postmodern way; the urns we set atop the pilasters, the barrel vaulted ceiling, and the contrasting pale gray surfaces and ebonized floor make the space feel like one of the remarkable passages in the Sir John Soane house museum in London. So as not to detract from its stately elegance, we added only the stool, and an unusual book table, with a gilded iron base from the 1930s and a pale celadon Corning glass top, on which sits, with perfect aplomb, a Giacometti ostrich.

"I want you to channel Myrna Loy" was my clients' delightful directive for their bedroom, and it doesn't get more explicitly glamorous than that. The room's centerpiece, accordingly, is the white-silk-wrapped bed that I designed to take advantage of four very beautiful rock crystal finials for which the couple had never been able to find a use. The finials' forms, the way they capture and reflect the abundant sunlight, find echoes in both the transparent elements of the vintage Bagues chandelier and the exceptional eighteenth-century mirror above

PREVIOUS: Alice Neel's portrait of the artist Red Grooms and his wife overlooks the living room from its position above the fireplace. I designed the Serge Roche–inspired upholstered chairs at left—the lotus-shaped gilt feet are a notable feature—and set a Jean-Michel Frank–style coffee table finished in gilded faux shagreen between them to infuse the space with a quiet glamour. OPPOSITE: A coffee table inspired by Jean Royère and a Claude Lalanne chair help to upend the room's built-in traditionalism.

The dining room is finished in a silvered monochromatic wallpaper from Gracie, with the palest possible blush of color evident in the butterflies and birds. The four carved consoles, based on an eighteenth-century English model, continue the wallpaper's motif in three dimensions.

the fireplace. As in the dining room, the near absence of color (the Venetian plaster walls are the palest shell pink) invests the space with a light, fresh atmosphere that balances the sensual luxury of the white fur rugs and ice blue hammered silk on the bergères and Jacques-Émile Ruhlmann–style chaise.

I have said that I suppressed my own impulse to dial things up in deference to the residents' preference for restraint, especially as regards color. But the house does contain one notable exception, a room as glamorous as a jewel box. It is the library, off the first-floor main hall, and its most singular feature is the paneling: turquoise walls given the reflectivity of glass through the application of some forty coats of Chinese lacquer. I wanted the color to exude a certain strength but didn't want the room to be so dark that it felt inviting only at night; because the walls absorb and radiate light, the library remains just as welcoming during the daytime (its reflective qualities are given an additional assist by the 24-carat water gilding on the handkerchief-vaulted ceiling, and the gleaming twice-ebonized floor). As the room's palette is otherwise a neutral ash brown, we developed a unique "book-matched" zebra rug, for which the hides were selected and stitched in a way that mirrors the book-matching ordinarily associated with wood veneer, a striking, almost surreal effect. It's not too much to say that the library is one of the most distinctive rooms my office has created: in a way over the top, yet with a balance and restraint that makes it easy and comfortable to inhabit—for me, the best kind of glamour there is.

In the end, this project taught me a great deal more than how to adjust my methods to suit a client. Rather, it opened my eyes to the fact that interior design really is an art form: not just a job to get done, as it can be for certain people, but a journey of discovery in which the participants play off of, and listen closely to, one another as together they breathe life into a dream. My clients questioned everything; edited each moment carefully, so as to clarify the design's delicacy without dispelling it; and embraced trial and error as an opportunity to hone the outcome to perfection. All of which added up to a wonderful collaboration, one that, not least, made me better at what I do.

A splendid lantern in gilt bronze, by the contemporary Parisian artist Louis Cane, hangs in the apple-green breakfast room, one of the few spaces in the residence strongly punctuated by color. Eighteenth-century English chairs surround the table; the plaster consoles date from the early twentieth century.

ABOVE: The second floor's rear stair hall is watched over, literally, by a Jean-Baptiste Huynh photograph.
OPPOSITE: The upstairs book room features a table combining a base attributed to Maison Ramsay with a glass top manufactured by Corning, for which the means of production no longer exist. An ostrich by Giacometti sits atop the table. The urns atop the pilasters contain up-lights, which impart a gentle glow to the handkerchief-vault ceiling.

The principal guest suite features communicating sleeping and sitting rooms; the artist Paulin Paris created the playfully elegant trompe l'oeil motif. A Catherine Opie photograph, from the artist's Ice House series, hangs above the sofa, creating a "window" that extends the space. The circa-1920s "draped" console contributes to the suite's sense of whimsy, as does the appliqué, also by Paulin Paris, above it.

ABOVE: The larger of the guest suite's two bathrooms features a triptych mirror with concealed medicine cabinets to the left and right. The gray-and-white marble pedestal sink was custom crafted for the room. OPPOSITE: The sitting room, off the master bedroom, features a canvas by the Los Angeles artist Billy Reynolds with a palette entirely in sympathy with the mauve walls and floral-patterned eighteenth-century Aubusson rug. The silver gilt frames of the 1940s chairs are combined with coffee and side tables by Bagues from the same period.

I was reluctant to answer my clients' request for a red library, not wishing to compete with the legendary one designed for Brooke Astor by the great Albert Hadley in the 1960s. So we migrated the color into a guest bedroom. Louis Cane, the Parisian artist who created the lantern in the breakfast room, designed the superbly crafted desk, with its ingenious mechanisms, lacquer finish, flower motif, and gilt bronze frieze—all of it the acme of chic. The settee is by Andrée Putman.

ABOVE: The bay window belongs to the library; the terrace above it is off the master bedroom. OPPOSITE: The pool house is accessed via an underground photo gallery, and draws in abundant sunlight from the oculus window. Tables from the postmodern design collective Memphis are paired with 1940s club chairs found in Paris.

ABOVE AND OPPOSITE: The chairs, dining table, and console were designed and custom-crafted for the loggia, sited between the library and dining room. I mounted a collection of jade disks from China on stands to create an interesting all-weather arrangement of objects that serves as an abstract counterpoint to the terra cotta figures. OVERLEAF: The gilt bronze bird is by Claude Lalanne.

THE GRAND TOUR

WHEN I FIRST MET THE RESIDENTS OF THIS HOME, THEY DESCRIBED THEIR FANTASY OF LIVING IN A PLACE THAT DREW THEM BACK INTO THE EIGHTEENTH CENTURY. WHAT THEY DIDN'T REALIZE WAS HOW DEEPLY IN THE PERIOD THEY COULD ACTUALLY IMMERSE THEMSELVES—AND I HAD NO IDEA THAT I WAS ABOUT TO EMBARK ON ONE OF THE MOST EXTRAORDINARY ADVENTURES OF MY PROFESSIONAL LIFE.

A WELL-ESTABLISHED AND SUCCESSFUL COUPLE, THEY'D MOVED FROM SAN ANTONIO TO ATLANTA TO BEGIN A NEW PHASE OF LIFE, AND DECIDED TO USE THE OPPORTUNITY TO REALIZE A LONG-CHERISHED DESIRE:

PREVIOUS: The center hall links the entrance and front of the house to the garden and pool in the back. The limestone and Belgian black floor inserts are typical of an eighteenth-century chateau or *hôtel particulier*. The hall includes a collection of mostly French and Italian eighteenth- and nineteenth-century furniture and objects, including a remarkable group of antique silvered bronze and steel pistols. OPPOSITE: The salon features Louis XV–style paneling by Féau & Cie, painted and gilded by Atelier Mériguet, both in Paris.

PREVIOUS, OPPOSITE, AND ABOVE: The salon's furniture is principally eighteenth-century French. Notable pieces include a pair of gutsy, large-scale Louis XVI girandoles from the Wildenstein Collection; four Régence appliques; and a pair of rock crystal, amethyst, and smoky quartz chandeliers. However, the coffee table—though the top is an eighteenth-century lacquer panel—was made by Jansen in the 1950s, and the rug is a copy of an eighteenth-century Aubusson, executed in New York by Beauvais Carpets.

to live in an American version of a *hôtel particulier*, a grand mansion of the sort that flourished in prerevolutionary France. They were planning a 10,000-square-foot, four-story version of their dream in an enclave of town houses, in Atlanta's Buckhead district, modeled on the Place des Vosges; when the couple explained to their architect, Peter Block, what they had in mind for the interior, he suggested they sit down with me (thank you, Peter).

Ours proved to be an intriguing first meeting, straightforward but with an excitingly unexpected undercurrent. The couple visited Paris multiple times a year and had developed a love and appreciation of French arts and culture; they imagined a home drawing decoratively on a span of roughly seventy-five years, from the Régence period through the reign of Louis XV. This in and of itself wasn't all that unusual. What proved different was that the couple weren't drawn to typically classical eighteenth-century objects but rather to stronger, more exuberant things, which is very much my own taste. While they'd been thinking strictly in terms of furniture, they also had, I saw, a great curiosity about what else might be done, and how we could work together to achieve something special. Most of all, I felt their level of commitment—they were not only willing but eager to go on a journey.

What my soon-to-be clients *didn't* know was that the environment we could create went beyond furniture to a total aesthetic embrace of the world of the Bourbon kings. I suggested that we go to France, the better to show them the possibilities—and they accepted without hesitation.

For aficionados of boiserie—historic French and European wood-paneled rooms—Féau & Cie, in Paris's seventeenth arrondissement, is the ultimate destination. Guillaume Féau has amassed a collection that includes more than a hundred entirely intact paneled rooms from the seventeenth and eighteenth centuries, as well as fragments and drawings of many more, and when I brought my clients to his atelier, the experience proved transforming. Working with my Paris associate Hina de Laubriere, I'd combed Guillaume's collection, selecting

Atop the eighteenth-century Louis XV mantelpiece, I placed an arrangement of some of the treasures found on our grand tour: a gilt bronze Louis XVI clock, English blue john and gilt bronze urns, and beautiful mounted eighteenth-century Meissen cachepots, all discovered in Paris and at The European Fine Art Fair (TEFAF) in Maastricht.

installations from different periods and choreographing them in sequence, to demonstrate how they might unfold in the couple's home. When they understood that Féau's artisans, trained in woodworking traditions going back hundreds of years, could re-create these historic chambers in Atlanta—that the surfaces with which they lived could be so authentic—the pair embraced this comprehensive approach completely. My clients' fantasy became my own, mine became theirs, and it all coalesced into a grand vision, one that went well beyond what any of us had imagined.

My first step, reworking the architectural plan, had less to do with any shortcomings than the fact that when our clients began design development with Peter, there wasn't yet a cohesive idea driving the overall residence; once all of us had a clear picture, we were able to develop fewer rooms with grander proportions, which could accommodate what we intended to accomplish. I followed the revised architectural plan with a very complete furniture plan, indicating where everything from hallway pedestals to living room settees to dining tables to beds would be placed. This is standard practice—it's the way an interior designer determines a room's requirements—but a tight furniture plan remained especially important in this case: Rather than a simple shopping trip, my clients and I were proposing to take off on what amounted to a grand tour.

Every really successful project, in my experience, results from a collaboration between myself and the people whose home I'm designing. I am extremely enthusiastic about what I do and have a passion for pushing things as far as they can go, for fine-tuning a room until it sings, and I'm never satisfied until I know a design is there (and sometimes not even then—there's "there," and then there's "*there*"). In this case, I found myself working with two people whose energy and enthusiasm equaled my own, who were determined to make the time to pursue the incredible things we hoped to find. And (with apologies to Humphrey Bogart) we also had Paris: At that time, the city still offered a relative abundance of important, unusual eighteenth-century furniture that was also reasonably affordable.

Atop the gates surrounding the town square of Nancy are a series of distinctive urns made of tole. Over time, some had been removed and replaced with new ones, and my clients and I came upon one of the originals at the Paris Biennale. Shortly after the purchase, my Paris office discovered a *second* one, in the atelier of one of my restorers, who'd done work in Nancy nearly four decades earlier. Now both urns stand atop pedestals flanking the entrance to the dining room.

OPPOSITE: The second-floor stair hall extends from the salon past the dining room, to an antehall that connects to the library. The table is a true treasure: a very-late-seventeenth-century Louis XIV giltwood piece, topped by two Imari vases with gilt bronze bases and a large eighteenth-century marble covered tureen. A mid-eighteenth-century Louis XV tortoiseshell and gilt bronze clock is suspended above the stair; the lantern dates from the same period. ABOVE: In the antehall off the kitchen, paintings depicting scenes from Aesop's fables. The change from stone to wood floors signifies the transition from the more public setting of the hallway to the intimate library experience.

And it wasn't just Paris. Over five years, the three of us made thirty-five trips, ranging in length from three days to a week, and went everywhere and anywhere beautiful things could be found—London, Rome, Florence, Brussels, Antwerp, Maastricht, and towns all over Europe. My office organized each excursion around regions that were particularly rich in one or another style or furniture type, or places where we'd pre-scouted pieces I felt my clients should see. And of course we were open to discovery every step of the way: I likened us to a trio of jazz musicians who knew the music but left ample room for improvisation. And like all simpatico players, we pushed one another to reach for new heights and go in multiple directions. It was a grand tour in every imaginable way.

Meanwhile, the workshops at Féau were producing wonders. A living room paneled in Louis XV boiserie, which had traveled across Paris to Atelier Mériguet-Carrère to be painted and water-gilded in 22-carat gold leaf. An octagonal Régence dining room, finished in peacock blue lacquer, inset with Chinese red lacquer and gilt decorated panels. A library antehall with boiserie featuring painted scenes taken from Aesop's fables—exact reproductions of originals in Guillaume's collection but scaled to fit the space. Once they were installed, the outcome was almost eerie in its accuracy: Before we'd added a stick of furniture, the spaces exuded a palpable sense of history.

As for that furniture: Since we'd opted for exuberance and originality rather than strict traditionalism and had hunted in so many different parts of Europe, the collection proved to be a lively, surprisingly prismatic view of the eighteenth century, a big idea, interpreted in multiple ways. For the living room, we found an unusually large Louis XV giltwood canapé, so generous in its proportions that it conforms to modern standards of comfort. Atop a boldly sculpted console table in the master bedroom, we set a contrastingly restrained eighteenth-century Italian traveling dressing table, a piece that finds an echo in a delicate Régence writing table that came from a dealer in Brussels. Thanks to a wonderfully individual selection of objects, notably the Régence giltwood armchair and black lacquer *bureau plat*, and a Louis XV *fauteuil de bureau* that's scaled for a woman,

The Louis XIV–inspired library, designed and crafted in French oak by Féau & Cie in Paris, incorporates modern amenities: the false-book door at left conceals a television; the one on the right hides a humidor. The coffee table combines a Maison Ramsay–style base with a porphyry marble top. A Régence trictrac table stands between two eighteenth-century armchairs at left.

The doors on the bar cabinet, which were incorporated into the design for the room, are eighteenth-century raised Chinese lacquer; they belonged to me, but had never left the Paris workshop of Ateliers Brugier, as I'd never been able to find an appropriate use for them. Brugier, which since the 1920s has produced extraordinary lacquer restorations and furniture, crafted the cabinet to complement the doors without competing with them.

the Directoire paneled master sitting room became a place in which it's a pleasure to spend time. And though it is sparsely furnished, the master bath's late-seventeenth-century carpet strikes just the right note—it's exactly what Louis XIV would have had.

But the most challenging part of the project wasn't finding the right objects for every purpose, or ensuring that, at every scale, the commitment to quality was absolute. It was, rather, bringing a continuity to the residence that made it appear to be the product of a single sensibility. Just as an orchestra conductor fuses multiple players into a single voice, my job was to ensure that everyone involved, whatever their talents as soloists, was telling the same story. There is a difference between filling beautifully crafted historic spaces with precious things, and creating a unified home; achieving that quality of singlehandedness took all my skills.

Fortunately, it worked. As I'd had the complete trust of my clients, we'd purchased many things not on the furniture plan, once-in-a-lifetime pieces we couldn't bear to pass up. But in fact the installation proved to be the most extraordinary I'd ever done: From the moment we began setting up the rooms, the design sprouted wings and soared, the great abundance of everything we'd discovered coming together with a beauty and unity that was breathtaking.

The thing I'm most proud of is how well the house captures my clients' sensibilities. For all the finery on display, it has nothing to do with show-and-tell; the couple continue to derive pleasure and satisfaction from what, in the end, is their creation, a home that grew out of their own interests, enthusiasms, and fantasies, and reflects them in every particular.

It was one of the most wonderful rides of my life. And, actually, we still have a small shopping list. Of course, if you walked into this house and I said, "We're still looking," you'd think we'd lost our minds. But the tour continues.

The dining room's décor was inspired by the Régence style, but the reality is more of an aesthetic bricolage drawing together multiple elements: mirrored surfaces, red Chinese lacquer with gold decoration, peacock-blue boiserie, and a Tiepolo-style ceiling. The seventeenth-century chandelier (which pairs gilt iron with rock crystal), the Louis XV console table, and the girandoles all derive from the same period.

OPPOSITE: Embossed painted and gilded leather covers the walls in the antehall leading to the master suite; the eighteenth-century portrait of Louis XIV is executed in embossed leather as well. The paneled doors, so rich in appearance, are in fact faux-painted by the artisans at Mériguet. ABOVE: Treillage-patterned inset lacquer panels—inspired by European lacquer at Pavlovsk Palace—distinguish the small powder room on the first floor. The eighteenth-century chandelier with Meissen flowers and the pair of sconces harmonize with the surfaces perfectly.

ABOVE: The Louis XVI–style bed was designed specifically for the room: it's of a size that didn't exist in the eighteenth century. The paintings over the bed and on the door to the lady's bath belong to the residents' collection of seventeenth- and eighteenth-century fan projects, one of the largest collections of its kind in the world. ABOVE AND OPPOSITE: The Louis XV–style boiserie in the master bedroom gives way to the more neoclassical Directoire paneling in the adjoining sitting room. The bedroom contains a collection of exceptional eighteenth-century furniture from different but related genres. Gianluca Berardi of Macondo Silks executed the exquisite embroidery on the curtains; their couture quality invests an already thoughtfully considered space with an even greater level of detail.

OPPOSITE: A Régence armchair and a Louis XV *fauteuil de bureau* face each other across a black lacquer *bureau plat*.
ABOVE: The eighteenth-century beaded panel above the effervescent Régence table in the bedroom rises up to reveal a television. The object below it is a folding dressing table used for travel—a noblewoman's version of campaign furniture.

OPPOSITE AND ABOVE: The lady's bath and dressing room, with polychromed boiserie taken from a Louis XVI original, partners well with the Calacatta Gold marble on the floor, tub deck, and vanity top.

OPPOSITE: A Chinese-inspired hand-painted wallpaper from Gracie, with a lilac background, establishes the tone of relaxed elegance in a guest room off the garden. The Louis XVI bronze and crystal chandelier and black lacquer *bureau plat*, and the Chinoiserie valence above the French doors, add grace notes. ABOVE: A richly patterned Calacatta Paonazzo marble floor enriches a guest bath.

The veranda, off the ground-floor central hall, features eighteenth-century-style Portuguese tilework commissioned by my office, enlivened by hunting scenes. The beautifully crafted, colorful nineteenth-century wicker chairs were found in Paris; the companion sofa is contemporary. The room, which features three large sets of doors opening onto the terrace and garden, remains relaxed and cheerful no matter the season.

ABOVE: On the house's top floor, exposed reclaimed wood beams convey the sense of an attic garret; the change enabled us to tone down the richness a bit and create a satisfying contrast, almost a country-house feeling. The seventeenth-century-style parquet d'Arenberg floors—similar to parquet de Versailles, but less formal—contribute to the mood. OPPOSITE: The guest bedroom, at the end of the long hall, nicely balances the rich and the rustic, with its sculpted limestone fireplace and eighteenth-century chandelier (originally destined for the master bedroom, until an even more spectacular one supplanted it).

SEASIDE ECHOES

PLANNING A GRAND NEW HOME ON A MAGNIFICENT PIECE OF PROPERTY (THAT YOU'VE ALREADY BEGUN TO LANDSCAPE) ISN'T THE IDEAL WAY TO DISCOVER THAT YOU REALLY WANT TO LIVE SOMEPLACE ELSE. BUT SOMETIMES EXPERIENCE IS INDEED THE BEST TEACHER, AS IT PROVED TO BE FOR THIS HUSBAND AND WIFE. THE COUPLE HAD FOR MANY YEARS MADE THEIR HOME IN AN OLD MANUFACTURING CITY IN SOUTH CENTRAL NEW YORK, AND DECIDED TO BUILD A FEDERAL-STYLE MANSION THERE, ON A HIGH OVERLOOK WITH SWEEPING VIEWS. MY OFFICE WORKED WITH THE ARCHITECTURE FIRM, FERGUSON & SHAMAMIAN, ON DEVELOPING INTERIORS FOR THE CLASSICAL RESIDENCE, AND THE BLUEPRINTS PUT ONE IN MIND OF

Mount Vernon; the landscaping had the quality of an Edwardian English park. It was a superlative combination, but in the course of design development, the couple began spending time on the south shore of eastern Long Island; as they came to realize how much they enjoyed this sylvan region, it became apparent as well that the husband didn't have to live where he worked. And so—bravely, I think—the plug was pulled on the grand estate, and the pair began house hunting in towns along the Atlantic.

The search yielded a big Shingle Style residence, light-filled and open to the outdoors, on an especially felicitous site—across the road from a farm field, adjoining a protected natural landscape, and within hailing distance of a bay: rural and agrarian, with the aroma of the sea. The architecture was quite traditional, as were the couple's tastes and lifestyle, so it was a good fit. But they also understood that a new life opened the way to a different aesthetic, lighter, fresher and, for them, a bit of a risk. And so—again, bravely—they decided to embrace it.

As our discussions progressed, I came to feel that the décor should take its cue from both the immediate environs and the broader context of the region. Though it wasn't especially large (roughly an acre), changes to the landscaping, including reorienting the pool to set it elegantly on axis with the house's great room, made the property feel much more expansive, and my clients were eager to strengthen the relationship of the interior to the grounds. And though it wasn't on the beach, I wanted to create a connection, if only subconscious, to that experience. Accordingly, I considered each of the house's rooms from the standpoint of its relationship to the outdoor space it adjoined or overlooked, creating a varied interior design, each part of which contributed to a shifting narrative that embraced the garden, the sun and sky, and the sea.

The story begins, appropriately, in the double-height entry hall, which with its grand stair, heavily paneled walls and ceiling, and three-sided second-floor landing enclosed by balusters, felt very old-world. To give it a more contemporary vitality, I worked with the artist Bill Sullivan to create a dramatically organic chandelier,

PREVIOUS: To enliven the somewhat formal, rectilinear architecture in this double-height entry hall, I introduced organic elements that evoked—in some cases explicitly—the residence's close proximity to the sea: a three-tiered chandelier that captures the motion of the waves, an ornate nineteenth-century Georgian-style console with fluid lines, and a mirror framed by seashells. OPPOSITE: Ornately carved Portuguese chairs with cushions upholstered in an antique ikat contribute to the spirited mood.

made from plaster-coated resin, with three tiers of great, swirling wave forms, elements that inject a palpable sense of nature and movement into the rectilinear space. On the wall below these surging waves I set an outsize mirror, its frame and crown formed from arrangements of seashells, above a gessoed mahogany George II–style console from the nineteenth century, with cabriole legs that seem to dance in sympathy with the mirror's tentacle-like shapes. The composition—decoratively extravagant, bold enough to hold its own in the soaring space, and entirely high-spirited—establishes the house's tone and serves as a prelude to what follows.

I stuck with these rhythms in the formal dining room, directly off the entry and overlooking the house's landscaped forecourt. Bill Sullivan was again recruited, to create the base of the circular table, another swirling form resembling a rocky, windswept outcropping; above the parchment tabletop, I hung an eighteenth-century Italian chandelier that has the lightness and whimsy of spun glass. A substantial mirrored buffet, inspired by a Serge Roche original, captures and reflects the abundant sunlight that fills the room throughout the day. And rather than hanging pictures, we turned the entire room into an installation, commissioning the Brooklyn atelier Point 618 to create wall-size murals that have the depth and fluidity of Monet's water lilies, executed in a play of blue and lilac that spills gracefully onto the upholstered dining chairs and cascades down the curtains. The room is relaxed, but with an elegance that bridges the gap between a casual weekend house and a more formal dwelling; the sense it conveys, of an organic island form awash in a sea of light, color, and motion, is a natural continuation of the spirit of the entry.

I knew the couple would gravitate to the great room, which despite its designation is actually a relaxed space that's open to the casual dining area and big kitchen. But I wanted to make sure they'd use the more buttoned-up living room, which looks out onto a lovely corner of the back garden and echoes the afternoon sun. The room, unfortunately, suffered from architectural issues that worked against its potential, notably unusually high

I continued the seaside motif in the dining room (off the entry hall) with a table, designed by the artist Bill Sullivan, that echoes the swirling movement of water and wall murals based on Monet's water lilies, the colors of which flow into the upholstered chairs and curtains. The porthole mirror, flanked by 1940s beaded glass and amethyst sconces, reflects an eighteenth-century Italian chandelier.

wainscoting, which made all the furniture feel disproportionately low, and an even higher massive stone fireplace that gave the naturally light, bright space an oppressive quality.

Again collaborating with Ferguson & Shamamian (recruited to make numerous alterations to the house), we stripped away the wainscoting, and I covered the walls with a white wave pattern formed from cast-in-place wet plaster—a fun gesture, bordering on kitsch, that's about as far from my clients' traditional style as they could possibly have imagined—and replaced the stone mantel with a simple, sleek fireplace surround made from cast glass bolection molding backed with mercury. The transforming effects of these changes were profound, and I supported them with a decorative element, by a Japanese textile designer, that I'd always wanted to use: translucent curtains with fringes of coconut woven into the fabric, which gives them the appearance of Persian lamb. I love the way the texture works with the wavy walls, and the fringes glow with sunlight like soft, exposed filaments. Though the furniture, much of which we designed for the room, is grown-up in style and arrangement, it's a delightfully comfortable and welcoming space to inhabit. There's a spontaneous, atmospheric canvas by Sophie von Hellermann, at once abstract and figurative, that we found for the room, the title of which captures the mood perfectly: *Please Don't Forget to Tip the Waiter.*

Another painting, this one belonging to the owners, influenced my thinking about the master suite and enabled me to inject the spirit of the seashore into the design. It's a colorful, slightly naïve waterscape that brings to mind Raoul Dufy's joyful, sketchbook-style 1929 watercolor *The Bay of Angels,* showing the beach and promenade at Nice; and since the couple's second-floor private rooms not only overlook all the garden but also enjoy a long, sky-filled view toward (in my imagination, at any rate) the ocean, I wanted the suite to have the flavor of the Côte d'Azur, that region's indelible combination of pleasure, art, and serenity.

We began by replanning the spaces to suit the way the couple live: To one side of the capacious sitting room

Wave-patterned plaster walls helped transform what might otherwise have been a for-company-only living room into a relaxed and welcoming gathering place (abetted by white mink and silk pillows and a silk-and-hemp key-patterned carpet). The curtains, woven from strands of coconut fiber, capture and glow with the abundant afternoon sunlight. Sophie von Hellerman's canvas *Please Don't Forget to Tip the Waiter* injects a strong note of playful exuberance.

OPPOSITE: We replaced the living room's overscaled (and overbearing) stone fireplace with a discreet cast-glass surround. The work on paper is by the German artist Michael Krebber. ABOVE: My office designed almost all of the furniture in the room, including the Jean-Michel Frank–style coffee table.

Though it communicates directly with the living room, the library expresses a very different character. We removed a wall of bookcases, which had made the space awkwardly narrow and hard to furnish, and refinished the existing pine paneling to infuse it with greater warmth; the iron-and-onyx coffee table, nineteenth-century Indian carpet, ikat pillows, and calfskin-upholstered chair—not to mention Josh Smith's abstract canvas—all contribute to the library's slightly exotic eclecticism.

that forms the suite's introduction, a guest bedroom became a his-and-hers dressing area as sizable and well-appointed as a boutique; in the other direction, we added a breakfast bar off the bedroom, and paneled the too-plain wall on which the bed would sit, giving it texture and organization. Decoratively, the bedroom is a mélange of simple objects from varying periods—light-colored, reflective, transparent, textural—enjoying discreet relationships with one another. There's an eighteenth-century Swedish secretaire that references the shape of a mid-twentieth-century mirrored commode; the shagreen Samuel Marx–inspired night tables find an echo in the rice paper covering the fireplace wall, tinted a turquoise that appears in the Murano chandelier. With its high ceiling that follows the slope of the roof, the room feels incomparably soothing and peaceful. Relax on the chaise beneath the garden-facing windows, and the mind produces the sound of slow-moving breakers.

If there's one room with which I'm particularly pleased, it is, ironically, the one with no view at all—indeed, with no windows. It's the basement-level media/game room, aka the Rat Pack Room. I've often said that to focus exclusively on the impact that a space's decorative components will deliver can be misleading, because the artworks invariably change so much, and this room demonstrates the point. It contains a number of effective elements: a grass cloth wall covering and hemp carpets introduce texture; warmth derives from camel and harbor-fog blue tones; the furnishings range from simple to standout pieces like a pair of vintage Deco club chairs and a cabinet finished in book-matched crotch-grain walnut. But what ties it all together, and gives the lair its swank, sexy charge, is the collection of black-and-white photographs of show-business icons—Jayne Mansfield with Sophia Loren, Jean-Paul Belmondo, Tyrone Power, the Beatles, various James Bonds, and of course Sinatra and his posse—that we pulled together from multiple sources and hung salon-style all over the walls.

Like all the rooms in the house, this one offers its own specific pleasures. And even though you're below ground, a lightness of spirit nicely refers you back to the light-filled experience up above.

The great French furniture designer Gilbert Poillerat, who specialized in ironwork, strongly influenced my designs for the table and chairs in the kitchen, where the couple spends much of their time. The articulated ceiling and cabinetry details give the big multi-use space an organizing, and soothing, rhythm.

As it's directly on axis with the front door and pool, and connects to the kitchen via a large aperture, the family room gets more use than any space in the house. The custom-designed bench, with its integrated tray, is perfect for perching or putting your feet up, and establishes the relaxed, practical tone. Though I placed several antiques in the room (notably the Art Deco table in the left foreground), I deliberately excluded anything fancy.

The relatively nondescript architecture in this second-floor guest room needed a strong dose of magic. For inspiration, I turned to the work of the artist and theatrical designer Christian Bérard (1902–49), who most famously created the sets for Jean Cocteau's film *Beauty and the Beast*. The floors, painted a bright and shiny white, contrast appealingly with the texture of the hooked rug.

ABOVE: A grotto chair in the master bath. OPPOSITE: A pair of compelling horse photo-portraits by Bob Tabor against a pink-and-gray-striped wall treatment in the ladies sitting room.

What previously had been a nondescript basement zone was transformed into an unexpectedly swank media room with a collection of mostly black-and-white vintage photos of Hollywood notables, musicians, and sports figures, displayed salon-style. I also warmed and vitalized the room by introducing a range of textures, notably the reproduction of a midcentury Swedish rug and checkerboard-patterned grass cloth on the walls. Though it's casual, the room is punctuated by objects and artworks, like the canvas by Jacqueline Humphries, which prevent it from becoming too complacent.

HARMONIOUS COMPLEXITY

I'VE LIVED IN THIS 2,000-SQUARE-FOOT TWO-BEDROOM APARTMENT FOR THIRTEEN YEARS, BUT I MOVED INTO THE NEIGHBORHOOD—THE VERY HEART OF MIDTOWN MANHATTAN, TWO BLOCKS SOUTH OF CENTRAL PARK AND ACROSS THE STREET FROM CARNEGIE HALL—MORE THAN TWO DECADES AGO. SOME PEOPLE THINK I'M CRAZY, AS IT'S SO IN BETWEEN COMMERCIAL AND RESIDENTIAL, AND THE TOURIST AND BUSINESS STREET TRAFFIC IS INTENSE. BUT I'VE ALWAYS LOVED THE AREA'S PERPETUAL IDENTITY CRISIS—SO VERY NEW YORK—AND THE PLEASURES OF THE PARK, SURELY THE GREATEST TO BE FOUND IN ANY CITY, ANYWHERE. MAYBE ONLY SOMEONE WHO GREW UP IN MARYLAND CAN EMBRACE THE MIDTOWN BUZZ. BUT TO ME, IT'S ALWAYS FELT LIKE HOME.

And for my first eleven years, I had a fantastic apartment exactly one block to the north, on the opposite side of Seventh Avenue. Also very New York—everything leaked, including the ceiling—but super-Parisian, too, with big arched French windows that captured stunning park views. The place was on the twelfth floor (12A, to be precise), and I used to sit on the sofa and look across Seventh to the building I'm in now and think, "What wonderful big windows." Other than the glazing, however, it looked so plain from the outside, I never gave it a second thought.

Until I started hunting for a place to buy. I liked the informality of Manhattan's Upper West Side and had been looking there for several months, when one day a huge banner appeared on the building with the big windows, announcing luxury prewar apartments for sale. I studied the place more closely and discovered that the structure, designed by the influential architecture firm Warren and Wetmore (co-creators of New York's Grand Central Terminal) and completed in 1922, was actually quite handsome. So I crossed the threshold—and the moment I entered the very pure and spare Art Deco lobby, it was love at first sight.

As for the apartment, it proved ideal in many ways. I discovered a wonderful arrival sequence, with almost thirty feet between the front door and the living room. The architects had thoughtfully considered the plan, so that the bedrooms were completely separate from the public rooms (effectively in their own wing), and you could access the kitchen from the gallery, which meant you didn't have to carry your groceries through the living and dining rooms to put them away. Though management had renovated the kitchen and bathrooms inexpensively, the outcome was serviceable, and they'd installed the New York–apartment version of the Holy Grail—a washer/dryer—in the maid's room. The place had eastern, western, and northern exposures, so it received copious amounts of natural light. And in the well-proportioned rooms, I found that the windows were indeed enormous—almost seven feet high. There were a few drawbacks, of course. But I didn't need to look at the apartment twice to know that I'd struck gold.

PREVIOUS: A Kati Heck painting, *Der Neue Tafelrunde* (2007), hangs in the intermediate hallway, the second of three consecutive spaces that form the entry sequence. Because the space widens, I created a break by adding two sets of rusticated casings (with concealed closet doors between them). OPPOSITE: The northwest corner of our living room has an oblique, but nonetheless delightful, view of Central Park.

Though I moved in quickly, without making any structural changes to speak of, I knew I wanted to both update the interior architecture and give it more clarity and character. This was particularly the case in what might be described as the apartment's preface. When you open the front door, you step into a thirteen-by-six-foot space that was once part of the public area by the elevators; next follows the original vestibule, off of which the bedrooms are located; then the hallway widens a bit before arriving in the living room. When I first saw the place, the flow of these contiguous spaces was disrupted by a series of unnecessary doors, and I planned to make the hall feel more capacious and create a sequential entrance experience. Accordingly, I painted the initial space a dark, glamorous gunmetal blue-gray, then replaced the doorways in the apartment's hallway with rusticated pilasters that give the "beats" of the procession into the living room a strongly articulated cadence. Elsewhere, most of the details got redone as well—the cornices, baseboards, hardware, window and door casings—and I raised the door heights, which had the effect of making the rooms feel larger. I also found an eighteenth-century Italian marble mantelpiece at John Hobbs's gallery in London: neoclassical but masculine and gutsy, and the perfect size for the living room.

When I tell people that I actually didn't have a big fantasy about how I'd decorate my apartment if one day I owned one, they take it with a grain of salt, but it's true—I'm like the shoemaker whose kids went barefoot. Nonetheless, the

When I first painted the living room ceiling chocolate brown, I thought I'd made a terrible mistake—until the carpet from Beauvais, which features a seventeenth-century Mughal pattern, arrived and miraculously made it work. The space is divided into three sitting areas: two, anchored by sofas, on either side of the fireplace, and a third showcasing a superlative midcentury Italian desk. The painting above the marble eighteenth-century Italian fireplace, *Chador 33* (2000), is by Michael Krebber. The early-twentieth-century bronze lantern on the ceiling was made in Germany.

124

ABOVE, CLOCKWISE FROM UPPER LEFT: *Ovalo*, a marble sculpture by Maria Gamundi. A nineteenth-century Grand Tour copy of an ancient Roman foot, beside eighteenth-century Dutch andirons. A work on paper by Mimi Lauter sits atop a small Régence *bureau plat* finished in black lacquer and red leather. A Lalanne gueridon entitled *Singe aux Nenuphars*—a rare collaboration between husband and wife François-Xavier and Claude—beside an early Empire chair, one of a pair. OPPOSITE: A Joseph Kosuth neon artwork above a "Michael Roth" photograph by Robert Mapplethorpe. On the desk's other side, *Untitled* (2008), by Günther Förg.

interiors strongly reflect my sensibility, and my partner Danny's as well, the living room in particular: It's a scrapbook, filled with furniture, art, and objects gathered over nearly thirty years of enthusiastic collecting; the space wraps itself around me in a bear hug and I feel very comfortable and at home there. (I've intensified the feeling, I should add, by keeping the entry sequence cooler and more stripped down, a quiet simplicity that precedes the more luxe, layered atmosphere of the living room.)

Throughout the apartment, you can see as well my interest in mixing materials and varying shapes so that rooms don't speak a single language, and in creating juxtapositions of different periods and styles—intriguing collisions that highlight the connections and oppositions between classical and modern pieces, and the often subtle influence of the former on the latter. And there is what I like to think of as my fearless use of color, evident in the Tiffany blue (more or less) guest bedroom, and the mink-y mocha lacquered Venetian plaster swathing the dining room, which makes such a versatile background for art. (I *say* "fearless," but after I painted the living room ceiling a shade called Mississippi Mud, I told Danny it was the worst decorative decision I'd ever made in my life, until the boldly patterned brown-and-white carpet came in and brought it into balance—and then I thought, "home run.")

I'm always reminding clients, when I make preliminary presentations, that the essence of a design scheme can't be entirely captured by the fabrics, carpets, or curtains, the qualities of the surfaces, or even the furniture or decorative objects. All that is significant—but it's the art that really gives an interior design its zing. That's something I always strive to achieve in my work, and it proved no less important in my own home.

Truthfully, it's not too much to say that Danny and I are art-crazed, and in fact a motivating factor behind my choice of the apartment was that it had a lot of wall space. And we've filled it, with paintings and artworks of every sort; while we don't focus on a particular style—there's everything from the very figurative to the wildly

On either side of the portal to the dining room, we placed two of our most prized possessions: a pair of bronze crocodile consoles by Claude Lalanne. The second of the pair of Empire chairs, upholstered in a velvet fabric designed by Jacques-Émile Ruhlmann, is at the left side of the portal.

abstract—a number of German artists are represented, among them Kati Heck, Michael Krebber, Albert Oehlen, and Michael van Ofen. Photography, too, plays a strong part, a fact made manifest by the ten-foot-long Richard Misrach beachscape in the entry hall; in the master suite, the bed is flanked by intimate abstracts by Brett Weston and Minor White, and a fantastic "installation" image of a building under demolition by the French photographer Georges Rousse hangs above; and there's a sweet, eloquent picture of two kids sharing a tub, by Nicholas Prior, in the guest room.

I've collected sculpture, too: My favorite is a small, quite remarkable nude by the Costa Rican artist Maria Gamundi in white marble, which can be set in multiple poses and works beautifully in all of them. And our beloved Lalannes, which straddle the line between furniture and sculpture. We have a small table that represents one of only three collaborations between the husband-and-wife creators: Claude did the "ginkgo" top and François the "monkey" base. And two "crocodile" consoles by Claude flanking the entrance to the dining room: The day they arrived, I would have to say, was the most exciting art-related moment of my life.

Danny and I make sure to keep the hanging pieces moving, too, as they change in character from place to place, and the rooms themselves transform as canvases come and go, combine and recombine. The Mel Bochner "word" painting got bumped into the dining room when a Krebber took its position above the fireplace, but it looks even better in its new location—and got better still when an abstract Oehlen came in and highlighted its graphic qualities. I probably shouldn't say this, but there's no more exciting way to redecorate than to change around your art.

Did I mention that my current apartment is also 12A? Yes: I can look north across Seventh Avenue and see the windows out of which I once looked at the windows I look out of now. Such a short distance—but what a great and satisfying journey.

The dining room walls are surfaced in a mocha Venetian plaster with a lacquer finish on top, by artist Mark Giglio, which gives the color a surprising luminosity. The large canvas to the right of the window, *No* (2009) is by Mel Bochner; to the left, *Mannetje-Vrouwtje*, a work by the Dutch artist Marc Goethals.

OPPOSITE: Photographs by (from left) Nicholas Prior, Alessandra Sanguinetti, and Loretta Lux in the Tiffany blue guest room. The leopard-print carpet is an affectionate nod to the great French designer Madeleine Castaing. ABOVE: A chair by Hubert le Gall in the third section of the entry, before a ten-foot-long beachscape by the photographer Richard Misrach.

OPPOSITE: The Campana Brothers created the bronze chair in the master bedroom; the surrealist apple, entitled *Pomme Bouche*, is by Claude Lalanne; and Kati Heck did the work on paper above the étagère. The small painted ceramic sculpture, *Little Rondo on Three Feet*, is by Rodney Alan Greenblatt. ABOVE: The nineteenth-century bench at the foot of the bed, finished in a gilt shagreen, was found in Antwerp. Photographs by (from left) Minor White, George Rousse, and Brett Weston. Isamu Noguchi designed the lantern.

AMERICAN SPLENDOR

OF ALL THE MANY PLEASURES TO BE FOUND IN *THE GREAT GATSBY*, ONE OF THE KEENEST IS F. SCOTT FITZGERALD'S DEPICTION OF GATSBY'S HOME IN THE FICTIONAL TOWN OF WEST EGG: A GRAND WATERSIDE MANSION, FILLED WITH FANTASTICALLY DECORATED ROOMS OF EVERY SORT, ALWAYS OVERBRIMMING WITH LIGHT, MUSIC, AND GUESTS, AND WITH A VIEW ACROSS THE WATER TO THE MAGICAL LIGHT AT THE END OF DAISY BUCHANAN'S DOCK.

GATSBY'S PLACE COMES READILY TO MIND WHEN YOU VISIT THIS 30,000-SQUARE-FOOT LOUIS XVI–STYLE CHATEAU, DESIGNED BY THE ARCHITECTURE FIRM KEAN WILLIAMS GIAMBERTONE AND COMPLETED SEVERAL YEARS AGO, ON LONG ISLAND'S NORTH SHORE. SET ON ROUGHLY THREE ACRES, WITH A FORMAL PARTERRE OFF THE LIVING AND FAMILY ROOMS OVERLOOKING A POOL AND, JUST BEYOND IT, THE WATERS OF THE SOUND, THE HOUSE CONTAINS MAIN-FLOOR ROOMS THAT TAKE THEIR STYLE AND SCALE FROM THE EIGHTEENTH CENTURY,

PREVIOUS: A pair of eighteenth-century German commodes flank the portal to the salon in the double-height entry hall. ABOVE: For the draped table across the entry hall, we fabricated an appliquéd and embroidered fabric finished with gold and silver metallic threads; the mirror above it is mid-eighteenth-century Régence. OPPOSITE: The Tiepolo-inspired ceiling painted was executed in Paris on canvas and installed by artisans from Atelier Mériguet. Above the superb Louis XVI canapé, attributed to Jacob, a view of the Champs-Élysées and its environs, circa 1850.

a lower-level grand ballroom (opening onto an indoor pool) that has the flavor of the Belle Époque, and bedchambers of a more contemporary intimate scale up above. It is lavish in every way; yet, unlike Gatsby's hectic Jazz Age energy, a surprising restraint, even a stillness, to the atmosphere is welcoming and soothing.

This, I think, derives from the residents, people with classical tastes who enjoy an exceptionally refined way of life and maintain their home impeccably. They came to me for a design that drew inspiration from prerevolutionary France, and we hit it off beautifully; yet I understood that the quality of restraint that gave the couple distinction required me to exercise a comparable impulse: rein in my attraction to exuberant forms and layering of multiple elements, and develop a quieter interior design that hewed more closely to tradition. At the same time, my clients' love of the refined detail—which I very much shared—encouraged me to invest their home with the singularity and elegance of haute couture.

I mean that literally. Two things differentiate rooms done in the style of eighteenth-century France from their original counterparts. The first is the way the furniture is arranged. The second is the introduction of luxurious upholstery, and it was here (and in other elements, such as the curtains, requiring embroidery) that I was able to bring to the design a special frisson, by working with Parisian artisans who do embroidery for the major fashion houses. My love of exuberance and layering notwithstanding, the fact is that chateaux, whatever their grand present-day connotations, were essentially country homes, simple and relatively austere, in which the pleasures of food, wine, and nature were foregrounded. By keeping the décor comparatively restrained, and focusing on the beautifully crafted, highly finished detail, I was able to provide a gracious stage on which the family's life might play out.

This was the case with all aspects of the design—I worked, as my office often does, with Atelier Mériguet-Carrère on the painting and gilding, and Féau & Cie crafted some of the boiserie. But we also found multiple opportunities to develop embroidered elements that were as far from prêt-à-porter as you can imagine. As per

From the dining room antehall, a view through the entry to the stair hall off the library. Objects include a beautifully crafted Louis XVI lantern, a mirror from the same period, and a pair of late-eighteenth-century neoclassical urns that we lit from within. The gilded armchairs flanking the console, two of a set of four, are copies of early Empire originals that complete the dining room seating.

tradition, I wanted to keep the vast two-story entry hall sparsely furnished, and so installed little more than a pair of eighteenth-century German commodes and a large Régence mirror; since I didn't want a third important furniture piece, I covered the new draped wood table beneath the mirror with an appliquéd and embroidered cloth drawing on seventeenth-century motifs (thereby introducing a different kind of craft into the space). In the living room, the exquisitely designed and sewn feather patterns on the double-sided seat before the fireplace—which we refer to as the Baby Jane back-to-back pouf—were carefully drawn and templated prior to execution, so that they fit precisely as planned; the room's window shades—with leaf forms in appliquéd gilded leather, combined with gold elements and embroidered silk—required extensive preplanning to ensure that the multiple elements fell properly. In some instances, the workshops chose to do mock-ups in flannel as a trial run: With pieces this complicated, it can't be a guessing game.

Of course, in a house so big, incorporating so great a variety of experiences, I find it useful to change the mood when appropriate, and the downstairs ballroom enabled us to shift away from the royal court of France and go in a more whimsical direction. We wanted a Beaux Arts richness and opulence, with some of the flavor of the old Paris opera—my male client loved the idea of the men drinking at the big walnut bar and observing the action, as in a Degas or Toulouse-Lautrec—and so the masters from Mériguet arrived from Paris and finished the entire room in faux marble and porphyry; the twin fireplaces, copied from a Napoleon III original, were sculpted by two teams, first in China, then in France, over a period of eight months. Rather than lighting the enormous space with wall sconces, which would simply have gotten lost, I added a layer by ringing the room with marble columns topped by eighteenth-century girandoles. We also had fun with the walls of the indoor pool area, decorated with eighteenth-century-style Portuguese tiles, and hung a William IV chandelier in the vaulted "wine lounge" the family uses for intimate dinners: Both gestures give us a bit of respite from the arts of France.

The Louis XVI doors to the salon were created by Féau & Cie based on originals at Versailles; Atelier Mériguet executed the finishing and gilding. In the foreground, a painted and gilded Louis XVI armchair stands before a Régence *bureau plat* in black lacquer, gilded bronze, and brass inlay. The carpet is an eighteenth-century Aubusson from Beauvais Carpets. Not everything, however, is French: the chandelier, in gilt bronze, cobalt blue glass, and crystal, hails from eighteenth-century Russia.

The fireplace is a copy of an Empire original; beside it stands a superb small secretaire with tambor doors that open to reveal a fitted interior; the small stool beneath it dates from the Régence period. The applique to the right of the mantel is an exceptional nineteenth-century copy of an even more extraordinary Louis XVI model at Versailles. The pillow fabric on the chair beneath it is a vintage Régence textile, found in Paris, that we used here and elsewhere in the room.

Féau & Cie crafted the mahogany library in Paris, where Atelier Mériguet executed the gilding and finishing—two of the world's great workshops collaborating to produce a magnificent example of the Empire style at its most pure. Mériguet also produced the Louis XIV–inspired ceiling; the chandelier is very-early-nineteenth-century Viennese. The chair to the right of the Louis XVI desk, one of a pair, is from the Directoire period; the table directly behind it is an incomparable Empire gueridon, finished in gilt bronze and with a marble top. As for the two large-scale Empire chairs before the fireplace: one is a copy of the other.

OPPOSITE: My favorite room in the house is the Wedgwood-blue and ivory dining room, executed by Féau & Cie in the Louis XVI style—an almost perfect replication of an eighteenth-century chamber. There are a few subtle differences, notably the surface-painted mirrors (as opposed to the more typical reverse painting), a technique developed originally to please Marie Antoinette. My favorite room also includes my favorite chandelier, a very-late-eighteenth-century gilt bronze Austrian object incorporating opaline glass, an amber dish, and stylized griffons—truly astonishing. ABOVE: The buffet is a copy of an eighteenth-century original in the dining room of Paris's Musée Nissim de Camondo. The chairs are decorated with symbols representing astrological signs.

OPPOSITE: The family room, with its richly finished pine paneling, is in the English style, and evinces a comfortable, clubby elegance. All of the upholstery is contemporary; the pillow fabrics were designed by Sabina Braxton. The chandelier is a nineteenth-century copy of a Louis XIV model, and a particularly good one. ABOVE: A Napoleon III cabinet, in the style of Louis XIV, topped by a *very* Restoration clock.

ABOVE: A delicate Gracie wallpaper in Ming green sets the tone in the wife's study. The unusual green Wedgwood chandelier reflects the palette of the room and is an eye-catcher, as is the crisp Directoire fireplace. OPPOSITE: The master bedroom is a neoclassical composite. The starting point is the eighteenth-century Italian trumeau mirror, in the Louis XVI style, above the fireplace; the carving is of an exceptional level of quality, and the blue, gold, and ivory color palette completes the piece beautifully. The unusual eighteenth-century Swedish chandelier features cobalt-blue églomisé panels decorated with cherubs; the square form of the bottom is mirrored. The bed is a copy of one of Marie Antoinette's; the trunk at the foot of it, built in Paris by Mériguet, is finished in painted and gilded embossed leather with nailhead trim; a television rises from within when the lid is raised.

CLOCKWISE FROM TOP LEFT: A Louis XIV chandelier, very late seventeenth century, in glass and gilt iron. A detail of the salon fireplace. The casing around the dining room doors. The festoon shades in the salon, appliquéd, gilded, and painted leather with embroidery.

CLOCKWISE FROM TOP LEFT: One of a pair of German neoclassical chandeliers in the ballroom. A window at the top of the entry hall stair. The window treatments in the bedroom. A detail of a painted mirror in the dining room.

OPPOSITE: One of the panels in the ballroom. A very exuberant Louis XV Rococo console with a marble top, one of a pair, harmonizes with the faux porphyry pilasters, gilding, and faux marble, all executed in bravura fashion by Mériguet. ABOVE: The stair, which descends from the first-floor library gallery, leads to the ballroom. The overscaled neoclassical console, finished in white and gold with blue accents, is what I'd call Kentian, Italian-style.

The ballroom fireplaces are copies of a Napoleon III original, and were executed in France. This image gives a sense of the ballroom's grand scale, and reveals the Louis XV–inspired Savonnerie carpets; early-eighteenth-century girandoles (a pair of originals, the others copies); and the rows of columnar pedestals on which they stand. Appliques on the wall would have gotten lost and robbed the room of dimension.

My absolute favorite room, I must confess, is the one that most closely reflects my own sensibilities—the dining room. It incorporates everything great about the eighteenth century and is the most finished of the house's multiple spaces. The carpet is a copy of one at Versailles (now in the collection at Waddesdon Manor) that was created for Louis XIV, and its vibrancy beautifully complements the room's color, a variant of Wedgwood blue. The walls themselves were painted and glazed, then stone-rubbed to create a patina—they're at once remarkably authentic and entirely luminous. The mirrors, palladium silver-leafed on the back, feature decorative painting on their surfaces, which creates a sense of depth not found in the more typical reverse-painted églomisé glass. On a visit with my clients to the Musée Nissim de Camondo, I suggested that a particular console there would be ideal for the dining room; we had it carved from marble by an extraordinary Parisian workshop that used the same stone selected by artisans in the 1700s. And suspended above it all is the chandelier to beat all chandeliers, an Austrian piece from the late eighteenth or very early nineteenth century with gilt bronze winged dragons surrounding an amber cut crystal bowl—without question, the most beautiful and unusual piece of its kind that I've ever put into an interior.

The house looks beautiful, and by no measure does it appear incomplete. But I'm glad that my clients have suggested, of late, that I might come back and add a layer or two. Nothing that contravenes the design's quiet spirit—just a little more. In the entry, paintings over the commodes, perhaps, and a tapestry above the grand stair. The mahogany-paneled library, a very masculine homage to the Empire period, could use an authoritative chair behind the desk, a second sofa table, and a taboret bench (and some art). And I can see a superb pair of brackets, topped with jars, by the living room windows, and barometers atop its mirrored panels. People sometimes ask, "How do you know when you're done?" The best answer I can give is that a design is complete when my clients feel utterly at home—and sometimes they have to live with it a bit to know if it needs another beat.

The wine lounge features a copy of a Louis XIV mantel, carved from the same stone that would have been used in the seventeenth century. The chairs are Italian Empire; the chandelier is a wonderful example of the William IV style. The painting, appropriately enough for a room devoted to the pleasures of the vine, is a portrait of Bacchus.

The spa room, as it's called, is in fact the joint between the ballroom and the indoor pool. The treillage gives the interstitial space the atmosphere of a garden room. The Louis XVI terra cotta dates from the eighteenth century; the chandelier is a tole and Meissen object from the same period.

PREVIOUS: The inset panels surrounding the indoor pool are copies of eighteenth-century Portuguese tiles. The furniture, other than the grotto chair, was designed and built for the space. OPPOSITE: The veranda, between the indoor pool and the house's rear garden, features an inlaid Syrian table and an eighteenth-century lantern.

TRADITION REDEFINED

THOUGH MY WORK IS ECLECTIC IN ITS EMBRACE OF MANY PERIODS AND STYLES, CERTAIN THEMES AND IDEAS APPEAR, IN ONE FORM OR ANOTHER, IN VIRTUALLY ALL THE ROOMS I DESIGN. REFLECTIVITY, FOR INSTANCE. I LOVE IT: I CAN ONLY IMAGINE WHAT IT MUST HAVE BEEN LIKE, IN EIGHTEENTH-CENTURY FRANCE, TO BE IN A GRAND SALON IN WHICH THE LIGHT OF A THOUSAND CANDLES WAS AMPLIFIED BY WALLS OF SILVERY MIRROR. FREQUENTLY, I LAYER TEXTURES AND PATTERNS, SOMETIMES BOLD AND GRAPHIC BUT MORE OFTEN QUIET AND SUBTLE; THOUGH SMALL AND SEEMINGLY

PREVIOUS AND OPPOSITE: For the long gallery off the entry hall, I commissioned a pair of Tron de Pauline bronze armchairs, incorporating ginkgo leaves, by Claude Lalanne. The graphic, midcentury-style painted floor, of our design, leavens the formality by introducing a lively, less traditional element, enhanced by the pair of zebra-skin rugs laid atop it. Two large-format architectural photographs by Candida Höfer (one featuring a vaulted ceiling similar to the one in the gallery) add contrasting depth to the linear layout.

still, they charge a space with tremendous energy. And whether it's a piece of furniture, an artwork, or even a bit of upholstery, I look at everything as an object, one with a shape or silhouette strong enough to hold its own in an aesthetic conversation without raising its voice. When properly handled, these three elements— reflectivity, texture, silhouette—can bring a room to life at any price point and invest the most ordinary architecture with force and glamour.

All of these elements came into play in a home nestled in an especially lovely part of Long Island's north shore, a region in which the thickly leaved branches of shaggy old trees make canopies over the roads, and proper Georgian manors from the 1920s and 1930s, some with their estates still intact, conjure up the flavor of a genteel, semi-rural past. My clients' home, though in fact it dated from the 1980s, was somewhat reminiscent of that old style, a kind of Norman-meets-Georgian hybrid, with a steep roof and white-painted brick walls, on four acres adjoining a country club.

It offered the promise of an enjoyable, easygoing life. But the owners—whose main residence, on Manhattan's Upper East Side, I'd designed previously—weren't of the same mind about it. The husband had grown up in the area and actually knew and admired the house as a young man; his parents still lived virtually around the corner, which offered their young children the pleasures of close-at-hand grandparents (while the adults visited the golf course directly accessible from the backyard, through the enormous rhododendrons). The wife, conversely, didn't think they'd really use the house all that much, as they already had two other "second" homes—one on Long Island's *south* shore.

No surprise: The couple asked me not to do too much and to keep the design simpler and more humble than in their luxurious city dwelling. Yet part of a designer's job—a big part—when clients aren't yet clear on what role a place will play, is to develop interiors that will help them make the home their own, to find ways to

In the bay window at the center of the gallery, directly opposite the front door, I placed a mahogany and gilt table dominated by a pair of whimsical, entirely unique candelabra, also by Lalanne; these create a translucent screen between the interior and garden view through the window.

get the most from it. And since the design directive involved keeping things relatively simple (at least at first), I used my three enduring interests as a bellows to bring the embers of the house's potential to life.

The entry hall, which unites the house's two wings and offers an expansive view of the garden, sets the tone. The first, and biggest, change I made was to the very blond, and very bland, parquet floor. I'm a big fan of patterned floors, and so I organized a stained and painted geometric design that worked with the rhythm of the parquet beneath it (then added a pair of zebra rugs for an extra layer of elegant exuberance). In addition to knitting the overall structure together more effectively, the design is more "mod" and bridges the gap between the house's traditionalism and the promise of a more contemporary way of living. The floor-to-ceiling picture window overlooking the garden, directly on axis with the front door, inspired me to introduce a pair of grand-scale Candida Höfer photographs (both of hallways) on the opposite wall: Architectural in character, they at once glamorize and extend the physical space and, like the new floor, oppose the air of tradition. While there's almost no furniture—I wanted the stripped-down flavor of a gallery—we commissioned a pair of stunning objects from the incomparable Claude Lalanne: two bronze Tron de Pauline chairs that are as big and imposing as thrones but much more piquant. If the overall effect remains high-key, it also reflects the fact that the owners are fun, young-spirited, and not afraid of shaking things up.

We migrated this stylish vitality into the living room with a slightly dimensional, not entirely even Venetian plaster shadow stripe on the walls (a surface that also creates luster without being overly shiny), and a jute rug that looks and feels easy and natural but has a strong, rhythmic geometry to the weave. Given my attraction to reflectivity, I love to design mirrors, and installed one above the fireplace with a distinctive watery border and a biomorphic shape that plays off the suave appliques, by the singular Parisian artist Hélène de Saint Lager, that flank it. The ceiling we finished in a highly reflective chocolate brown that firmly

One end of the living room, as seen from the antehall off the gallery. The Russian chair, which dates from the late eighteenth century, is one of a set of four; and the 1920s armillary, set on a Lucite stand that highlights its sculptural qualities, was found in Paris. The Asian lamps flanking the sofa were executed, with uncommon delicacy, in steel and brass.

resolved the room's architecture and created a background for the silhouette of the big lantern suspended in the center.

An interesting point about pieces, such as that lantern, with commanding profiles: In a space that texture has infused with nervous energy, the stillness of a compelling object gives the eye an opportunity to rest. The living room has two to which I'm especially drawn: a massive seventeenth-century Louis XIV console table, a baronial element that answered my male client's desire for a grand "English country house" experience; and an unusual 1920s armillary I found in Paris, and floated atop a Lucite pedestal, the better to cast it as a work of art. Speaking of art, the room's—indeed, the house's—major ooh-la-la artwork, a blazing wall-size abstract canvas by Lee Krasner, demonstrates something essential about both the art of decoration and the nature of collecting: I'd planned a room with very little color, but the beautiful, personal things you love always find a way in.

The house's weak link and, consequently, the one I most wanted to transform, was the confining, inexplicably trapezoidal dining room,

The living room's diamond-patterned two-toned hemp carpet gives the room a vibrant ground of color and texture. The walls, finished in a Venetian plaster with an irregular stripe, contribute to the background's quiet vitality. And the chocolate-brown ceiling adds a reinforcing form to the room's architecture and knits all of the surfaces together.

OPPOSITE: The wall lights, flanking a mirror of my own design, are by the Parisian artist Hélène de Saint Lager; Caio Fonseca created the small artwork beside the fireplace. ABOVE: A copy of a nineteenth-century Korean table; its lacquer finish incorporates an inky black into the dominant orange.

OPPOSITE: The big Louis XIV table is one of my very favorite objects of its kind—the scale is fantastic. And it pairs remarkably well with the equally commanding abstract canvas, by Lee Krasner, above it. It's unusual to find a wall big enough to support that scale of furniture and art, and I was happy to take advantage of it. ABOVE: The branch-form mirror is by Hervé Van der Straeten.

which along with its other problems had (thanks to the plunging roofline) an ungainly down-sloping ceiling. Once we repaired the architectural damage (by literally raising the roof), we developed what is unquestionably the residence's most glamorous finish, by first lacquering the walls, then lightly flecking them with dots of gold leaf, a technique that produces an extraordinary constellation pattern—it's like gazing at the Milky Way. To extend the space, and capture and reflect the walls, I again indulged my passion for mirror design, creating a contemporary version of an eighteenth-century Venetian looking glass, reducing the historic adornment to a simple, slender transparent bead between the beveled border and the antiqued plate. Another element that brings both strength and sparkle to an interior is metal, here represented by a pair of graceful ironwork sconces in the spirit of the twentieth-century French designer Gilbert Poillerat (the Paris studio where we had them fabricated is today overseen by the son of Poillerat's collaborator, which gives the fixtures an extra measure of authenticity). The room can't comfortably hold more than eight. Yet it has indeed been transformed, into an intimate, elegant chamber that shimmers with life.

I'm happy to say that, after we worked closely with the couple—helping them wrap their heads around how best to use the house and make it their own, and extending and encouraging that through design—their north shore residence is the "second home" they enjoy the most, both as a family space and as a pleasurable environment for entertaining. This partly has to do with giving the rooms a personality that reflects not only who my clients are but, more to the point, who they are in this particular context. But I also came to understand, as I developed the rooms' backgrounds, that the house had lacked cohesiveness; there wasn't a thread that began at the front door and wove its way through the entire place. With reflective elements and surfaces, layers of texture and pattern, and objects that announced themselves quietly but clearly, we were able to knit the house together into a consistent, very satisfying narrative.

A Poillerat-inspired table base (with a faux parchment top) finds echoes in the wall sconces and lantern. The Venetian plaster walls were flecked with gold after receiving a lustrous coat of lacquer; I designed the contemporary interpretation of an eighteenth-century Venetian mirror.

In the library, I added the tray ceiling, finishing it in planks, and raised the height of the garden doors to give the architecture more authority. The Peter Beard mixed media work above the sofa introduces a tribal sensibility, reinforced by the African masks, jute carpet, and zebra-patterned curtains. ABOVE: *Petite Fille à la Poule*, by Claude Lalanne.

OPPOSITE: In one of the two guest bedrooms, we applied a blocked stripe to the linen fabric on the walls, which gives it a painterly quality that's almost reminiscent of Morris Louis. ABOVE: The convex mirror, opposite the bed, is from the early twentieth century and helps to enliven what was originally a somewhat neutral space.

OPPOSITE: The second guest bedroom features twin beds of my design. The Venetian plaster walls incorporate a slightly pearlescent stripe; the mirrors above the headboards date from the 1930s, and bring in an extra measure of luminosity. ABOVE: We added a flokati pillow to the room's custom-designed chaise.

ARTFUL LIVING

WHEN I FIRST MET THE OWNERS OF THIS RESIDENCE, I REALIZED THEY'D MANAGED TO ACHIEVE SOMETHING THAT, IN MY EXPERIENCE, WAS TRULY SINGULAR: NOT ONLY HAD THEY PURCHASED A VERY DISTINCTIVE HISTORIC HOUSE, THE PAIR HAD WORKED WITH THEIR ARCHITECTS TO GIVE IT A DAZZLING NEW LIFE.

A U-SHAPED COURTYARD HOUSE IN THE REGENCY REVIVAL STYLE, COMPLETED IN 1938, IT WAS ONE OF VERY FEW CEDAR-CLAD RESIDENCES IN ITS REGION. THOUGH THE STRUCTURE HAD DETERIORATED OVER THE DECADES, THE ARCHITECTS HAD DONE AN EXCEPTIONALLY SENSITIVE JOB

PREVIOUS: The eglomisé walls by Miriam Ellner in the entry hall were inspired by a Tahitian pearl; accordingly, the palladium silver leaf behind the watery glass panels incorporates shades of gray and lilac. The satin-finished wood trim resembles faux ivory. The painting is by Robert Motherwell. ABOVE: The gallery forms the next beat, after the entry, in the house's procession of rooms. The bookshelves grew out of a desire to create a rusticate reinterpretation of eighteenth-century Italian architecture, but with a modern edge; the faux-stone plastered finish suits the vellum-covered books, Picasso plates, and textured objects.

of restoring the house to its "original" condition while also making sympathetic changes that rendered the plan more responsive to the residents' lifestyle. In addition to extending the kitchen and staff wing, the architects enclosed the central courtyard, converting it into a living room of palatial proportions—thirty feet square, with a twenty-six-foot-high ceiling—that forms the new nucleus around which the residence revolves.

And yet. The interiors, though they'd been developed by an accomplished design team, were somehow out of sync with both the architecture and the couple's intentions. I was invited to their New York home to discuss a new direction.

When I arrived at their apartment, and even before I met them, it was instantly evident that these were two very sexy, glamorous people. Decoratively, the place captured everything I love about eclecticism at its best: furniture and artworks spanning five centuries, every one spot-on and holding the others in exquisite balance. All the surfaces were beautifully considered and executed; it's not often one sees a home with that high a level of finish. And it was evident that, as patrons of the fine and decorative arts, they had a deep understanding of quality and weren't afraid to go the distance to achieve it.

We talked for nearly three hours, and what became abundantly clear was that—especially for the wife, who'd spent years struggling with the project—the idea of having to exert so much effort again was daunting. As it happened, I'd already made plans to be in the area the following weekend, and the husband said, "The house is yours. Let us know what you think."

That weekend turned into two and a half months, in which I visited the house repeatedly and imagined another life for it. I knew the design would draw on the 1920s and 1930s and play off the architecture, but I was searching for a larger intention. When I'm asked to explain my working methods, I find it difficult, because it has a lot to do with intuition. I am very attuned to the energy of a home, its innate nature and vitality, and if a

PREVIOUS: A gilded plaster applique by the contemporary Parisian artist Patrice Dangel, above a French chair from the 1940s. OPPOSITE: A detail in the living room.

PREVIOUS: A view of the living room as seen from the gallery. The Picasso above the fireplace is flanked by a single Jean Dunand screen that has been divided. Decorator Frances Elkins (1888–1953), whose work I greatly admire, influenced the design of the silver leaf doors. The Lucite, bronze, and glass console behind the sofa was created for the room. OPPOSITE: Artworks by Lee Krasner, left, and Adolph Gottlieb, right, on either side of the door to the gallery. In the foreground, a Maison Ramsay table atop a nineteenth-century Indian carpet from Beauvais Carpets. ABOVE: An exceptional and rare Eugene Printz *bureau plat* sits beneath an atypical work by Morris Louis.

residence has no energy, there isn't much I can do with it. But this one exuded it in abundance: The place had a soul and a voice. So all the time my staff and I were deciding what to add, crafting furniture plans and considering finishes, I was listening to that very resounding voice, which flooded me with inspiration.

Ultimately, the owners decided to proceed, but first they required a presentation, one that would convey, in concrete terms, how my ideas might play out. Presentations of this sort are, of course, standard practice: Before starting work, designers show clients photos, fabrics, furnishings, sketches, a whole host of things in multiple media that collectively make up a picture of what they're going to deliver. In this instance, however, I felt this couple needed and deserved something more. So my office filled two trucks with furniture and objects representative of our design direction, sent them to the house, and set up the principal rooms the way I'd conceived them in plan—a presentation, in three dimensions, that left not the slightest doubt as to how the couple's home would look, feel, and function. So extensive were our preparations that we covered a substantial portion of a living room wall with our preferred painting technique, and produced full-scale copies of the pair's artworks so that they could be seen, and considered, in situ.

The experience lasted two days and yielded one of the most gratifying responses of my working life. The morning after we'd finished, the wife said to me, "Last night was the first time in five years I've gone to sleep with a smile on my face." With that, we were off to the races.

Much of what I'd been pondering during the weeks of preparation involved the surfaces. I always say to clients, "The most important things are the backgrounds: They're the elements to which you're most committed, the foundation upon which everything else rests." In this house, though the palette would largely be neutral, I wanted the backgrounds to be charged with vitality, to seem to be drawing light from the sea and sky. And having seen what they'd achieved in New York, I knew I'd been blessed with clients prepared to fully embrace the possibilities.

Ruhlmann-style armchairs stand before a coffee table by Jean Royère; Diego Giacometti designed the lamp in the corner. A Helen Frankenthaler canvas makes an excellent foil for the Gottlieb.

of restoring the house to its "original" condition while also making sympathetic changes that rendered the plan more responsive to the residents' lifestyle. In addition to extending the kitchen and staff wing, the architects enclosed the central courtyard, converting it into a living room of palatial proportions—thirty feet square, with a twenty-six-foot-high ceiling—that forms the new nucleus around which the residence revolves.

And yet. The interiors, though they'd been developed by an accomplished design team, were somehow out of sync with both the architecture and the couple's intentions. I was invited to their New York home to discuss a new direction.

When I arrived at their apartment, and even before I met them, it was instantly evident that these were two very sexy, glamorous people. Decoratively, the place captured everything I love about eclecticism at its best: furniture and artworks spanning five centuries, every one spot-on and holding the others in exquisite balance. All the surfaces were beautifully considered and executed; it's not often one sees a home with that high a level of finish. And it was evident that, as patrons of the fine and decorative arts, they had a deep understanding of quality and weren't afraid to go the distance to achieve it.

We talked for nearly three hours, and what became abundantly clear was that—especially for the wife, who'd spent years struggling with the project—the idea of having to exert so much effort again was daunting. As it happened, I'd already made plans to be in the area the following weekend, and the husband said, "The house is yours. Let us know what you think."

That weekend turned into two and a half months, in which I visited the house repeatedly and imagined another life for it. I knew the design would draw on the 1920s and 1930s and play off the architecture, but I was searching for a larger intention. When I'm asked to explain my working methods, I find it difficult, because it has a lot to do with intuition. I am very attuned to the energy of a home, its innate nature and vitality, and if a

PREVIOUS: A gilded plaster applique by the contemporary Parisian artist Patrice Dangel, above a French chair from the 1940s. OPPOSITE: A detail in the living room.

I turned to Atelier Mériguet-Carrère in Paris, the fifty-year-old firm that draws on techniques from the previous three centuries to produce decorative painting, gilding, and finishes of the very highest quality. The great fun of working with Mériguet comes when I have an idea that's rooted in the past and want to reinterpret it into something contemporary; thanks to the atelier's extraordinary artisans, the spark that ignites my imagination can be translated, via a wealth of knowledge and experience, into an entirely unprecedented reality.

The great example of this is the library, a beautifully detailed oak-paneled room in which the wood lacked character and vibrancy; I had this call-me-crazy idea that it could be a Louis XIV–style gilded chamber, but in spirit rather than actuality. I described this to Mériguet, and we began to experiment, creating sample panels that were at first wildly off the mark but gradually found their way to perfection. Once we'd hit upon the recipe, a team of ten flew over from Paris and spent three months in the library, first wet-sanding and wire-brushing the walls to bring up the grain; then painting the oak a Pompeiian pink and applying a layer of palladium silver leaf over that; and finally patinating and antiquing it all, so that the panels radiated a rich, lustrous glamour. Not every major room in the residence received this intensive a treatment, but all have highly finished backgrounds that articulate their personalities.

I took a similar approach to the house's contents. As I put it to my clients, "The things you want to see here are the things you just don't see." Though the furniture included selections from various periods, the tone for the entire project was set by a single piece, the one that spoke clearly in what was, for me, the house's true voice. It was a *bureau plat* (writing table) of arresting beauty and authority, created by the great French designer Eugene Printz in the 1920s, and when the three of us found it in a Paris gallery, I recognized it as a turning point. I suggested to my clients that, while we'd been developing a mix of classical and modern

I set a ceramic bust by Georges Jouve atop a Lucite pedestal. The dimensional wall pattern, based on an African kuba cloth, was executed in Venetian plaster.

OPPOSITE: Chairs by Jules Leleu surround a table of my design in the dining room. The column screen frames a work by Robert Rauschenberg. ABOVE: I surfaced the dining room walls with wet-sanded, wire-brushed oak (to bring out the grain), then painted it an inky blue-black, after which the entire room was silver-leafed; we lightly engraved the lower panels and chair rail. The verso of the mirror above the chair also received a palladium leaf treatment.

pieces, committing to the *bureau plat* would move the design firmly into the twentieth century. And it did: The Printz proved to be the cornerstone of a collection of mostly prewar French classics by Arbus, Frank, Giacometti, Rateau, Royère, and others that invest what is essentially a second home with a level of style that—however relaxed and comfortable the overall mood may be—commands notice.

Though we had only twelve months from start to finish, the house's great energy seemed to infuse us all. Most impressive to me was that the couple, despite their previous misadventure, were able to involve themselves in the task with creativity, discernment, and joy. People unfamiliar with the trade often assume a decorator will impose a style or sensibility on them. In fact, the opposite is true: I am only as good as my clients. Here, they really stepped up to the plate, and the outcome—interiors that will reward expectations as long as the home is theirs—reflects that at every scale.

In addition to the elaborate treatment given the oak walls of the library, the pilasters and upper panels were inset with faux shagreen; a leathered glazed finish, behind the books, provides a lively shot of color to what was otherwise a very sober room. Furnishings include pieces by Adolf Loos, Jean-Michel Frank, Diego Giacometti, and André Arbus.

ABOVE: A Ruhlmann-inspired chaise fills the library's window bay, which receives a water view. OPPOSITE: The sconces on either side of the delightful Alexander Calder were designed by Philippe Anthonioz. The taboret seat is by Jean-Michel Frank.

OPPOSITE: My design for the secretaire executed in palm wood, leather, and bone was inspired by the work of Emile-Jacqués Ruhlmann and the deco-era atelier Dominique.
ABOVE: Though the fireplace is made of stone, we finished it in plaster to reference Giacometti— a way of taking the Georgian mantelpiece and bringing it into the twenty-first century.

ABOVE: The grand stair leads up to the second-floor guest hall. OPPOSITE: Do not mistake the treatment of the lady's powder room for wallpaper: The Venetian plaster is stencilled with moon-gold and inlaid with mother-of-pearl and abalone by Laura Bergman. The desk, by the artist Louis Cane, was commissioned for the space, and is paired with a silvered wood chair from the 1920s. Bagues created the chandelier in the 1940s.

OPPOSITE: The walls of the guest room stair hall are a patchwork of different applications of textured plaster, which create a compelling rhythm as one moves through the space. ABOVE: A Kees van Dongen hangs above the white onyx Directoire-inspired fireplace in the master bedroom.

OPPOSITE: The Serge Roche–inspired bed is finished in panels of antique mirror (including the faceted octagonal posts); the inside of the canopy and bedcover are embroidered in a sunburst pattern. The curtains—appliquéd and embroidered on voile over taffeta—are based on a design by Balenciaga. The nightstands are by Samuel Marx. ABOVE: The engraved plaster walls in the lady's master bath are based on a motif by Armand-Albert Rateau (1882–1938), as is the window shade.

OPPOSITE: The Chinese lacquered walls of the study were executed by Ateliers Brugier in Paris; the door casings and fluted frieze draw on the designs of Emilio Terry. The hand-painted curtains abstract the movement of water, and in fact are set at the horizon line of the room's ocean view. Richard Diebenkorn created the work on paper. ABOVE: A 1940s sculpture executed in wood, found in Paris, guards the door.

The family room, off the master bedroom (with its Balenciaga-inspired curtains), is presided over by a bronze and steel mobile by Alexander Calder. The brown, ivory, and robin's-egg blue palette is all-enveloping and cozy, an effect enhanced by a diamond-patterned cork floor. An eighteenth-century Italian gilt and silver leaf sunburst hangs above the television.

A large seascape by Alex Katz brings the outdoors into the second-floor guest sitting room.
Chairs by André Sornay surround the game table and stand atop a blue-and-white striped dhurrie
rug designed for the room. We used a simple glass bolection molding to create a mantelpiece.

We furnished the loggia, off the living and dining rooms, with an eclectic mix of simple stick furniture. The large mosaic is by Fernand Léger; the console beneath it is by Philippe Anthonioz, who also designed the lantern.

ALFALFA HOUSE

I FIRST BEGAN VISITING ULSTER COUNTY, ABOUT TWO HOURS NORTH OF NEW YORK CITY, BACK IN THE 1990S, IN WHAT NOW SEEMS LIKE ANOTHER LIFETIME: AS A HORSEMAN AND REGULAR PARTICIPANT IN SHOW JUMPING COMPETITIONS. THE TOWN IN WHICH I RODE EACH SUMMER WAS PRETTY RUN-DOWN, AND THE HUMID WEATHER DIDN'T HELP; HAVING LIVED PREVIOUSLY IN A VERY BEAUTIFUL, CULTURALLY RICH PART OF THE BERKSHIRES IN MASSACHUSETTS, ULSTER DIDN'T INITIALLY APPEAL TO ME. SOMETIMES,

KEEP THIS
PLAC CLEAN

however, a small shift in perspective can make an enormous difference. One weekend, friends in the area invited me to stay, and when I showed up at their nineteenth-century "eyebrow" Colonial home, with its commanding views of the Catskills, I knew instantly that this was the region for me. The combination of mountain vistas, wooded landscape, and a genuinely rural character made the Ulster County I hadn't known a place I'd be happy to put down roots.

My partner, Danny, actually wanted something closer to the beach but had graciously given in to my love of the country; to soothe his feelings, I'd assured him that we'd find a house near water or one with a pool. That's when events began moving in unexpected directions. We were introduced to a local architect who'd decided to subdivide what had been his family's farm into a total of seven properties, ranging from about four to sixty acres, and design and build houses on each. When Danny and I went up to have a look, this plan was near completion, with three houses finished and several more under construction. The one we saw was an immediate not-for-us, but the last undeveloped, sixteen-acre parcel lay directly across the road. Incredibly enough, the architect hadn't visited it yet, so I suggested that we drive over and check out the view to the west.

Stopping the car, as fate would have it, precisely where our house stands today, we looked through the windshield toward an incomparable, unobstructed panorama of the Shawangunk Mountains. Everyone was stunned . . . and I heard myself say, "Boy, it's going to be hard to beat this."

It was, in effect, the first thing we'd seen, on the first day we'd looked. And neither of us had any desire to build—Danny and I just assumed, like optimistic house-hunters the world over, that we'd discover a place encompassing everything on the wish list. But when we began investigating the historic farmhouses that occupied our fantasies, reality revealed small-roomed, low-ceilinged structures in poor condition, typically

PREVIOUS: In one half of the entry hall in our Ulster County, New York, home, a comfortable blend of disparate elements: a Louis XVI cabinet, at left; a 1940s console table, on the right; photographs of Danny and myself by Andy Diaz Hope, by the door to the stair hall; and an Ashcan School painting and a Mika Rottenberg work on paper. OPPOSITE: Looking the other way in the entry: *Planter of Seeds*, a work by American artist John Sideli, on an eighteenth-century sculpture stand; a nineteenth-century Renaissance Revival chair, beside a Louis XVI–style French-Algerian table; and a Chris Doyle watercolor opposite an Impressionist canvas I found years ago in Paris.

right on the road—and costing a fortune to boot. However cold our feet, it didn't take long to see that we'd gotten it right on day one, and there was nothing to do but put the shovel in the ground and get started.

The house's design and construction proved to be a bit of a battle with the architect. But ultimately we prevailed on the most important elements: a twenty-seven-foot-long unobstructed entry hall running nearly the house's full width, and with a broad portal opening directly onto the living room, on axis with tall windows overlooking that western view; beyond the living room, a wonderfully generous fifteen-by-thirty-four-foot back porch where we hang out all summer; and a three-bedroom-plus-study plan that's a bit more than we need but very comfortable. Danny and I also visited several historic farmhouses with simple vernacular elements, from which we derived a vocabulary for our home: two styles of window trim for the different floors, a grandly shaped surround for the living room entry portal that elevates its importance in the architectural hierarchy, and wide-plank heart pine floors with a transparent gray stain—all very austere, but with an honesty and elegance in keeping with the region's aesthetic traditions.

As for the interiors, Danny offered a single directive—"no European furniture"—that I chose to interpret as "avoid the high-style formality of our New York apartment." Plenty of continental things crept in; but there's a casualness to the way the design took shape, an unfussy, unself-conscious ease that suggests a home that came together over a number of years—which is in fact the case, as it's filled with the furniture and art we've gathered, separately and together, across decades of work and travel. The proof of my commitment to informality is the simplicity of the backgrounds, the precise opposite of my usual approach; I didn't want to challenge the green beyond the windows, or de-emphasize the personalities of the objects and pictures, with surface sumptuousness.

I've described Danny and myself as "art crazed," and with even more wall space than our New York apartment, and dozens of pieces in multiple media, the house is certainly Exhibit A. As interesting as the size

PREVIOUS: Over the mantelpiece in the twenty-three-by-thirty-four-foot living/dining room is one of our favorite paintings, *Les Bisch Ja Nich Im Stich III* (2002), by the German artist Michael Krebber. The nineteenth-century *suzani* draping the console table was purchased a year before we moved in; the iron and bronze folding table by the sofa is part of our collection of campaign furniture. I had the table, with a cerused oak top, made for the room. Atop the pedestal at left: an urn made of pinecone flowers—our first purchase for the house. OPPOSITE: The oak stool before the fireplace is similar to one designed by Rateau for a house in England. Our friend Joanne De Palma designed the bronze and oak bookshelves.

OPPOSITE: The view of the living room from the kitchen reveals a seventeenth-century Louis XIV chair that looks very stoic but is incredibly comfortable. ABOVE: A view across the dining table to an eighteenth-century Swedish commode, above which hangs a painting by the Cuban artist Nelson Diaz. The pottery lamps are 1930s French; Hervé Van der Straeten designed the gilt and patinated bronze applique.

and variety of the collection, I think, is the way it's deployed, with multiple artworks grouped and displayed to create zones, a series of overlapping experiences that shift the mood from place to place and reinforce the emotional temperature of each. Our stairway, with its three distinct zones, captures this perfectly. The ground-floor stair hall is crowded with an eclectic grab bag: wire-form bug sculptures in cases, framed vintage Fiorucci shopping bags, a Hubert Le Gall lamp—a sum more lively, various, and attention-grabbing than any of its parts, and a compressed continuation of the salon-style art treatment in the living room. The hall's compression becomes elongated, and gently simplified, as you move up the stairs and pass a single artwork: a text piece in mercury glass, by the American artist Robert Wynne, that spells out "SOON." This quieting of the mood peaks at the second-floor antehall, in which four large photographs are hung gallery style, and at roughly the same eye level, forming a contemplative aesthetic landscape that prepares you for the experience of the bedrooms.

This may come as a surprise, given that it is, after all, a country house, but for the fifteen months we were embroiled in design and construction, Danny and I were so preoccupied, we didn't even think about the grounds. It wasn't until we moved in that I walked onto the back porch on a spring day, looked out across sixteen acres of dirt, and thought, "Oh my God, what have we done?!" It was especially distressing because, coming from a very busy precinct of New York City, I wanted to create a cocoon of absolute, utter privacy in which we didn't see or hear anybody, and we were completely exposed. And then, as it was spring, the alfalfa began coming up—right to the back door. My first official act as landscaper was to buy a Kubota, a professional riding mower, and start hacking back the crop before it overwhelmed the house.

I began by working with a local landscaper, Marge Brower of Back to the Garden, to screen off the town road, just to the south of the property, with a line of mature Norway spruce. Then, over a long series of Sunday

An Emilio Terry–inspired table in plastered oak lives on our second-floor landing. The photograph, *Tiananmen Square, Beijing* (2002), one of a series documenting China's transition from old to new, is by Sze Tsung Leong.

In the master bedroom, we painted the window frames and trim a shade of ash to articulate the room's architecture. An eighteenth-century sculpture stand in the corner showcases a piece, *Honey Pine Cone of Smiles*, by the ceramic artist Kate Malone. The Louis XVI *bureau plat* between the windows was one of my very earliest purchases; the revolving desk chair, of the same period, came from Paris, as did the Empire armchair on the right and the Directoire armchair by the fireplace. The curtains feature a hand-painted African pattern that, with the jute rug, gives the room an elegant rusticity.

OPPOSITE: Though the nineteenth-century iron four-poster was made in France, we actually found it at an antique fair in nearby Rhinebeck, New York. Above the bed, *Ex-Libris (Wittgenstein's Gift)*, a work on paper by Joseph Kosuth; behind the lamp on the night table, a photograph of Venice by Willy Ronis. An antique *suzani* from Madeline Weinrib covers the bed. ABOVE: The master bath, with artworks by Jean-François Fourtou, Roland De Leu, and Kosuth; the whimsical chandelier was constructed by a New York artisan, Thomas Blake, from plumbing supplies.

What you are regarding as a gift is a problem for you to solve.
—*Wittgenstein*

mornings, I worked at the kitchen table with a sketch pad, drawing and redrawing what would come to be the master plan for the five acres surrounding the house that we'd chosen to landscape (the rest remains farmland). Directly to the west, off the back porch and visible from the living room, I sited an expansive circular lawn, set within a square and anchored at the corners by four sugar maples, at the center of which is a lotus pond. After that, Danny reminded me that our deal was, if we weren't going to be near water, we had to put in a pool; we set it out of view of the main public spaces to the north of the house, enclosed by a frame of hornbeam hedging (as is the entire landscaped precinct).

Over time, we added less formal layers, crafting lawns, sitting areas, and gardens; yet though there's a carefully considered structure to it, the use of billowy plant material such as grasses and curved, undulant borders makes everything feel less rigid, more natural and enveloping, like a series of secret spots that require exploration to yield their mysteries. In a way, it's the opposite of the house, in which the elements have strong individual identities; outside, everything feels soft and fluid, and right angles are few. I love it—it delivers just the privacy and peace I'd hoped for (but not *too* much peace: I do most of the hedge clipping and pruning, and all the big grass cutting, which delivers the Zen of Instant Gratification).

When I'm asked my philosophy of country living as it's expressed in this house, I respond with a single word: *relaxed*. It doesn't make people feel uptight; everything is in bounds, and you don't feel like you have to ask permission to go in or out and do as you please. And when people want to know if there's an interior design lesson, I offer another word: *curiosity*. I'm always encouraging clients to just go and look, at everything, because the more you're exposed to, the more willing you'll be to go in unusual, unexpected directions. Our place, I hope, expresses that curious sensibility. It's always evolving, and some things work better than others—but in a way, that's what makes it home.

Above the antique American iron bed in one of the guest rooms, a Juju headdress made from dyed feathers, from Cameroon. The "confetti" wallpaper was designed by Albert Hadley.

OPPOSITE: In the second bedroom, twin beds I had made based on a Directoire daybed purchased years earlier; the Swedish-inspired cherry desk is of my design. Photos by (from left) Mark Feingold and Tierney Gearon. The clock on the desk, which dates from the early nineteenth century, is set within a cannonball. ABOVE: An eighteenth-century Swedish commode, beneath a paper-framed mirror. Albert Hadley's "black rose" paper covers the walls.

OPPOSITE: We constructed a deep porch on the house's garden side, which serves as a gracious outdoor living room in the summertime. The nineteenth-century French lantern, made of tole, was a gift from a client.
ABOVE: In the garden, a copper armillary from Balsamo sits atop a nineteenth-century English limestone pedestal.

The view from the west, looking back toward the house. Our architectural inspiration was the humble Midwestern version of the Greek Revival style. At the center of the garden, anchored by four sugar maples, we placed a lotus pond, supported by four dwarf Japanese cherry trees. The garage, behind the house to the right, helps to shape the arrival sequence at the end of the driveway. FOLLOWING PAGES: My design for the hemlock pool pergola is based on one commissioned by Prince Charles for Highgrove House and created by Isabel and Julian Bannerman, two of my favorite landscape designers.

RESOURCES

LANDSCAPE ARCHITECTS:

Back to the Garden
www.backtothegarden.com

Edmund Hollander Design
www.hollanderdesign.com

Howard Design Studio
www.howarddesignstudio
.com

Wirtz International
www.wirtznv.be

ARCHITECTS:

Andrew V. Giambertone
Associates & Architects
www.giambertonearchitects
.com

Fairfax & Sammons
Architecture
www.fairfaxandsammons.com

Ferguson & Shamamian
Architects
www.fergusonshamamian
.com

Miller & Wright Architects
www.millerwrightarchitects
.com

Peter Block Architects
www.peterblockarchitects
.com

Robert A.M. Stern Architects
www.ramsa.com

Robert W. Anthony
Architects
www.rwa-arch.com

CONTRACTORS:

Bonner Custom Homes
www.bonnercustomhomes
.com

I.Grace Company
www.igrace.com

Interior Management, Inc.
www.interiormanagement
.com

Kean Development Company
www.keandevelopment.com

Livingston Builders Inc.
www.livingstonbuilders.com

Mark Brown
www.markbrownbuilds.com

Peter Cosola Inc.
718.392.4111

Taconic Builders, Inc.
www.taconicbuilders.com

Wright & Co. Construction,
Inc.
www.wrightand.com

ARTISANS & WORKROOMS:

A. Schneller Sons, Inc.
www.aschnellersons.com

Albert Menin
www.albertmenininteriors
.com

Atelier Mériguet-Carrère
www.ateliermeriguet.fr

Atelier Midavaine
www.ateliermidavaine.com

Atelier Seigneur
www.tapissier.fr

Atelier Viollet
www.atelierviollet.com

Ateliers Brugier
www.ateliersbrugier.com

Carlton House Restoration
www.carltonhouse.net

Féau et Cie
www.feauboiserie.com

François Xavier et Claude
Lalanne
www.jgmgalerie.com

Hélène de Saint Lager
www.helenedesaintlager-art
.com

House of Heydenryk
www.heydenryk.com

Irena Kelly Custom
Draperies, Slipcovers &
Pillows
845.446.0220

Jane Henry Studios
www.janehenrystudios.com

Jonas
www.jonasworkroom.com

Laura Bergman
917.476.0455

Louis Cane
www.louis-cane.com

Mark Giglio
212.431.8926

Mark Uriu
www.markuriuinc.com

Miriam Ellner
www.mirriamellner.com

Mirror Fair Inc.
www.mirrorfair.com

Patrice Dangel
www.alexandrebiaggi.com

Paulin Paris
www.paulin-paris.com

Philippe Anthonioz
www.philippe-anthonioz.com

Point 618
www.point618inc.com

Pollaro Custom Furniture
Inc.
www.pollaro.com

Premiere Painting
www.premierepaintingnyc
.com

Thor Edmundson
The Stoneman
845.477.0235

Vosges Inc.
www.vosgesinc.com

WP Sullivan
www.wpsullivan.com

VENDORS:

A&R Asta Fireplaces
www.astafireplaces.com

Barry Perry Mantels
www.barryhperry.com

Beauvais Carpets
www.beauvaiscarpets.com

Macondo Silks
www.macondosilks.com

Nancy Stanley Waud
Fine Linens
www.nancystanleywaud.com
310.273.3690

Patterson Flynn & Martin
Carpets
www.pattersonflynnmartin
.com

P.E. Guerin Hardware
www.peguerin.com

Sabrina Fay Braxton Textiles
www.sabrinafaybraxton.com

Sevres Porcelain
www.sevresciteceramiques.fr

Verrier Passementerie
www.passementerie-verrier
.com

ANTIQUE DEALERS & GALLERIES:

Adrian Sassoon
www.adriansassoon.com

Alan Moss
www.alanmossny.com

Alexandre Biaggi
www.alexandrebiaggi.com

Antichita Alberto Di Castro
www.dicastro.com

Aveline Antiquaire
www.aveline.com

Balsamo
www.balsamoantiques.com

Bernd Goeckler Antiques
www.bgoecklerantiques.com

Carlton Hobbs
www.carltonhobbs.com

Chalvignac, Paris
+33.1.42616007

The Chinese Porcelain
Company
www.chineseporcelainco.com

Cupboards & Roses Antiques
www.cupboardsandroses.com

Downtown Accord
845.706.1070

Florian Papp
www.florianpapp.com

Fouquet
www.parisantiques.com

Galerie Adriano Ribolzi
www.adrianoribolzi.com

Galerie Bazin, Paris
+33.1.42974092

Galerie Bernard de Leye
www.orfevrerie.be

Galerie Chastel-Marechal
www.chastel-marechal.com

Galerie François Hayem,
Paris
+33.1.42612560

Galerie Gerard Orts, Paris
+33.1.42894448

Galerie Hervouet, Paris
+33.1.42612418

Galerie Kugel
www.galeriekugel.com

Galerie Liova
www.galerie-liova.com

Galerie Monluc
www.monluc.com

Galerie Mougin
www.galeriemougin.com

Galerie du Passage
www.galeriedupassage.com

Galerie Perrin
www.galerieperrin.com

Galerie Prot, Paris
+33.142606671

Galerie Sylvain Levy Alban
www.levyalban-antiques-
paris.com

Galerie Vallois
www.vallois.com

Galerie Wanecq
www.wanecq.com

H.M. Luther
www.hmluther.com

Honourable Silver Objects
www.silverobjects.be

Jason Jacques Inc.
www.jasonjacques.com

J.M. Zeberg Antiques
www.zeberg-antiques.com

L'Arc en Seine
www.arcenseine.com

Liz O'Brien
www.lizobrien.com

Maison Gerard
www.maisongerard.com

Newel
www.newel.com

Objets Plus
www.objetsplus.com

Pelham Galleries
www.pelhamgalleries.com

Philipe Vichot Antiques
www.vichot.com

Ralph Pucci International
www.ralphpucci.net

Victor Werner
www.victorwerner.be

ART GALLERIES:

David Zwirner
www.davidzwirner.com

Friedman Benda
www.friedmanbenda.com

Greene Naftali
www.greenenaftaligallery.com

J.G.M. Galerie
www.jgmgalerie.com

Luhring Augustine
www.luhringaugustine.com

Marc Selwyn Fine Art
www.marcselwynfineart.com

Paul Kasmin
www.paulkasmingallery.com

Sonnabend Gallery
www.sonnabendgallery.com

Yossi Milo
www.yossimilo.com

ACKNOWLEDGMENTS

There have been so many who have contributed to my success along the way, and tremendous gratitude and thanks are long overdue to the many indispensable people who have guided me and allowed me to flourish in the world I inhabit today.

To Albert Hadley and Sister Parish, who hired me right out of Pratt and showed me how to take the first steps on my career path. Their unbridled enthusiasm and love for their craft left an indelible mark on my life as a decorator. It was Albert's trust, generosity, and encouragement that gave me the confidence to develop my own point of view and trust that I could hang my own shingle out the door twenty-two (GASP) years ago.

There is one person without whom there would not have been a book: my "husband," Danny, who pushed me off the cliff and onto this path. His perseverance and persistence took me outside my comfort zone and convinced me to finally record my work and made me see that there were indeed the makings of a book.

To my agent, Jill Cohen, whose belief in this project with her wonderful zeal and love of what she does, sold me on undertaking this labor of love. To the photographers Fritz Von Der Schulenburg and Francesco Lagnese for their collaboration and amazing talent. To Marc Kristal, whose genius transformed my mumbled thoughts into words and has given me an articulate voice. To Doug Turshen and Steve Turner, whose artistic vision has shaped the way for those who don't know me to now know me a little better. To Oscar Mora, Gina Humphries, and Beth Eckhardt for their magical floral arrangements. And of course to Dervla Kelly and Leslie Stoker at Stewart, Tabori & Chang as well as all who took this to print and presented it so effortlessly and beautifully. My eternal gratitude.

To my parents, Justin and Sally McCarthy, who opened my eyes to what really matters in life while giving me the space and confidence to spread my wings. It is their insatiable appetite and curiosity about different cultures that started me on my own journey of discovery in this world. To my sisters, Kate and Elizabeth, who saw me through thick and thin and whose support has never wavered, I love you!

To my Parisian muse, Hina de Laubriere, who for fifteen years has been a true collaborator and guiding light.

To my BJM Inc. staff, past and present, who grease the wheels and see to it that every detail is attended to. Rajni Albin, Amy Allison, Mark Barnett, Todd Bishop, Cailen Brower, Kate Gallimore, Caroline Holden, Robert Kirkland, Kristina Lifors, Stewart Manger, Melanie McKinley, Patricia Scharf, Rellie Seville, and Jacquelyn Van Eck. I am lost without them.

To Tom Buckley, whose collaboration in Los Angeles was greatly valued.

I am indebted to the editors, writers, and photographers who over the years have encouraged me and introduced me to their readers: Dara Caponigro, Carolyn Englefield, Margaret Russell, Nancy Novogrod, Doretta Sperduto, Newell Turner, Michael Bruno, Anita Sarsidi, Sabine Rothman, Michael Boodro, Robert Rufino, Howard Christian, Tony Freund, Stephen Drucker, Samantha Emmerling, Barbara King, Christine Pittel, Linda O'Keefe, Jorge Arango, Mitchell Owens, Romy Schafer, David Patrick Columbia, Sian Ballen, Lesley Hauge, Kate Bolick, Penelope Green, Julie Baumgardner, Max Kim-Bee, William Waldron, Sophie Elgort, Peter Murdock, and Thibault Jeanson.

To the architects who make my dreams come true and push and inspire me every day, Richard Dragisic, Oscar Shamamian, Mark Ferguson, Richard Sammons, Anne Fairfax, Robert Stern, Randy Correll, Doug Wright, Robert Anthony, Alexandre Gamelas, Brian Covington, Andrew Oyen, and Damian Samora.

To my dear friends and colleagues Renee Meyers, Marin de Laubriere, Nicole Brugier, David Amini, Marc Selwyn, Peter Wylde, Carolyn Thorson and Andrew Carduner, Joanne DePalma, Pamela Mullin, Cornelia Lauf, Nancy Stanley Waud, Michael Simon, Sylvain Levy Alban and Charles Garnett, Chip and Sharon Shirley, Michael Seibert, Marc Selwyn, Daniella Ohad Smith, Terry Vaughan and Ira Rubenstein, David and Jessica McMurray, Alicia Messina and Billy Jaeger, Antoine Courtois, Guillaume Feau, Laurent Gosseaume, and Dabney McAvoy for their gift of friendship.

Published in 2013 by Stewart, Tabori & Chang
An imprint of ABRAMS

Cataloging-in-Publication Data has been applied for and may be obtained from the Library of Congress.
ISBN: 978-1-61769-043-3

Editor: Dervla Kelly
Designer: Doug Turshen with Steve Turner
Production Manager: Tina Cameron

The text of this book was composed in Requiem and Engravers.

Printed and bound in Hong Kong, China

10 9 8 7 6 5 4 3 2 1

Stewart, Tabori & Chang books are available at special discounts when purchased in quantity for premiums and
promotions as well as fundraising or educational use. Special editions can also be created to specification. For
details, contact specialsales@abramsbooks.com or the address below.

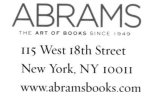

115 West 18th Street
New York, NY 10011
www.abramsbooks.com